A SIMPLE CHRISTIANITY

JOHN MACARTHUR

REDISCOVER *the* FOUNDATIONAL
PRINCIPLES *of* OUR FAITH

A SIMPLE CHRISTIANITY

Regal

From Gospel Light
Ventura, California, U.S.A.

Published by Regal
From Gospel Light
Ventura, California, U.S.A.
www.regalbooks.com
Printed in the U.S.A.

Library of Congress Cataloging-in-Publication Data
MacArthur, John, 1939-
[First love]
A simple Christianity : rediscovering the foundational principles
of faith / John MacArthur.
p. cm.
Originally published: First love. Wheaton, Ill. : Victor Books, c1995.
Includes indexes.
ISBN 978-0-8307-4754-2 (hard cover)
1. Jesus Christ—Appreciation. 2. Jesus Christ—Person and offices. I. Title.
BT304.5.M33 2009
232'.8—dc22
2008037995

2   3   4   5   6   7   8   9   10   /   15   14   13   12   11   10   09

Rights for publishing this book outside the U.S.A. or in non-English languages are
administered by Gospel Light Worldwide, an international not-for-profit ministry.
For additional information, please visit www.glww.org, email info@glww.org, or write
to Gospel Light Worldwide, 1957 Eastman Avenue, Ventura, CA 93003, U.S.A.

CONTENTS

INTRODUCTION

Loving the Lord Jesus Christ is what the Christian life is all about. If you are a Christian, you love Christ. Unfortunately your love is subject to fluctuation in its intensity. It takes a focused commitment on your part to love Him with all your heart, soul, mind and strength.

There is perhaps no better illustration of this waning intensity than what happened to the church at Ephesus, to whom Christ said, "I have this against you, that you have left your first love" (Rev. 2:4). The disease that plagued that congregation infects many contemporary churches. Instead of cultivating a deep and intimate relationship with Christ, many believers ignore Him, falling victim to the culture and turning to empty worldly pursuits.

I am so concerned that love for Christ not grow cold in the lives of Christians that several times throughout my ministry at Grace Community Church I have preached a message of warning from Revelation 2:1-7. This passage crystallizes the danger of becoming so busy in activity for Christ that one forgets the necessity of maintaining a rich, loving relationship with Him. The church at Ephesus had a great beginning. The apostle Paul invested three years of his life teaching the Ephesian believers the whole counsel of God (see Acts 20:27,31). Our Lord even commended the members for their service:

> I know your deeds and your toil and perseverance, and that you cannot endure evil men, and you put to the test those who call themselves apostles, and they are not, and you found them to be false; and you have perseverance and have endured for My name's sake, and have not grown weary. . . . You hate the deeds of the Nicolaitans, which I also hate (Rev. 2:2-3,6).

This was a noble group of people, who worked hard and persevered through difficulty. They established holiness and righteousness as their standard. Because their doctrine was solid, they recognized false apostles and avoided their influence.

In spite of their success, they missed the most important thing—they left their first love. Their labor of passion and fervor became cold, orthodox and mechanical. They left the heart out of their service—all their activity had become perfunctory. They believed and did all the right things, but did so coldly.

Like Ephesus, the nation Israel had been holy to the Lord at first. The Lord said to the people, "I remember concerning you the devotion of your youth, the love of your betrothals, your following after Me in the wilderness, through a land not sown" (Jer. 2:2). But then He said, "What injustice did your fathers find in Me, that they went far from Me?" (v. 5)

The honeymoon ended in Israel; it ended in Ephesus as well. Love turned cold is the forerunner of spiritual apathy, which then leads to a love for the world, compromise with evil, corruption, death, and finally judgment.

Can you imagine how you would feel if your husband or wife suddenly announced to you they didn't love you anymore, yet they still planned to live with you, sleep with you, and that nothing would change? Likewise you wouldn't ever dream of telling the Lord you didn't love Him like you once did, but that you still planned to come to church to serve, sing, give, and worship Him. May I suggest, however, that many of you do just that, only you don't realize it. That's the danger of spiritual apathy.

The apostle Paul never forgot the value of his relationship to Christ: "Whatever things were gain to me, those things I have counted as loss for the sake of Christ. More than that, I count all things to be loss in view of the surpassing value of knowing Christ Jesus my Lord, for whom I have suffered the loss of all things, and count them but rubbish so that I may gain Christ" (Phil. 3:7-8). Knowing Christ was his passion. For him nothing in life could capture his allegiance and devotion as much as Christ—not even his Hebrew heritage.

Ironically, Paul wanted to elicit the same love and devotion from the Ephesian believers. That's why he reminded them of their resources in Christ (see Eph. 1). We can't be sure how much they depended on Christ, but it must not have been enough since our Lord had to command them to "therefore remember from where you have fallen" (Rev. 2:5). A new generation had now risen in Ephesus that held to its strong tradition but not to an intense love for Christ. It's possible some were not even believers. Puritan Thomas Vincent recognized what a lack of love to Christ represents:

> The life of Christianity consists very much in our love to Christ. Without love to Christ, we are as much without spiritual life as a carcass when the soul is fled from it is without natural life. Faith without love to Christ is a dead faith, and a Christian without love to Christ is a dead Christian, dead in sins and trespasses. Without love to Christ we may have the name of Christians, but we are wholly without the nature. We may have the form of godliness, but are wholly without the power.[1]

On the other hand, a true Christian is evident by his consuming love for Christ. Vincent continues:

> If He has their love, their desires will be chiefly after Him. Their delights will be chiefly in Him; their hopes and expectations will be chiefly from Him; their hatred, fear, grief, anger, will be carried forth chiefly unto sin as it is offensive unto Him. He knows that love will engage and employ for Him all the powers and faculties of their souls; their thoughts will be brought into captivity and obedience unto Him; their understandings will be employed in seeking and finding out His truths; their memories will be receptacles to retain them; their consciences will be ready to accuse and excuse as His faithful deputies; their wills will choose and refuse, according to His direction and revealed pleasure.
>
> All their senses and the members of their bodies will be His servants. Their eyes will see for Him, their ears will hear for Him, their tongues will speak for Him, their hands will work for Him, their feet will walk for Him. All their gifts

and talents will be at His devotion and service. If He has their love, they will be ready to do for Him what He requires. They will suffer for Him whatever He calls them to. If they have much love to Him, they will not think much of denying themselves, taking up His cross, and following Him wherever He leads them.[2]

The Christian life is a continual pursuit of a deep, intimate relationship with Jesus Christ. Because he is committed to Christ, the true Christian will do nothing to dishonor Him. Instead he will look to Him for mercy and grace when he sins. He will seek His strength during times of trial and temptation. And he will desire His wisdom and knowledge to lead him through the maze of life's confusing circumstances.

That's my goal for you in this book. Like our Lord's instruction for Ephesus, you need to remember what you have in Christ and what He has accomplished for you. In the following chapters you will see Christ once again, as the God of the universe, as your loving Savior who willingly became a man to redeem you from God's wrath, and as the sovereign Lord who rules every part of your life. Hopefully this will rekindle your first love.

But our Lord's instruction for the church at Ephesus didn't stop with His command to remember. He also said, "Repent and do the deeds you did at first" (Rev. 2:5). Remembering who He is and how He has blessed you is not enough—you need to turn that knowledge into action. Without making a concerted effort to change your direction, you'll never deepen your relationship to Christ. Jettison the excess baggage you've picked up along the way and once again give Christ first place in your life. Don't "be led astray from the simplicity and purity of devotion to Christ" (2 Cor. 11:3), but exercise "love from a pure heart and a good conscience and a sincere faith" (1 Tim. 1:5).

Notes

1. Thomas Vincent, *The True Christian's Love to the Unseen Christ* (Ligonier, PA: Soli Deo Gloria, 1993), p. 1.
2. Ibid., pp. 1-2.

PART ONE

JESUS OUR GOD

THE PREEMINENT ONE

The One who is the object of our love was born contrary to the laws of nature, reared in obscurity, lived in poverty, and only once crossed the boundary of the land in which He was born—and that in His childhood. He had no wealth or influence, and had neither training nor education in the world's schools. His relatives were inconspicuous and uninfluential.

In infancy He startled a king. In boyhood He puzzled learned doctors. In manhood He ruled the course of nature. He walked upon the billows and hushed the sea to sleep. He healed the multitudes without medicine and made no charge for His services.

He never wrote a book, yet if everything He did were written in detail, the world itself couldn't contain the books that would be written. He never founded a college, yet all the schools together cannot boast of as many students as He has. He never practiced medicine, yet He has healed more broken hearts than doctors have healed broken bodies. Throughout history great men have come and gone, yet He lives on: Herod could not kill Him, Satan could not seduce Him, death could not destroy Him, and the grave could not hold Him.

But when the question is raised about who Jesus Christ really was, the debate continues to rage on as it has for nearly 2,000 years. Cults and skeptics offer various explanations. Some say He was a religious fanatic, a fake, or a political revolutionary. Others say He was just a good teacher. Still others take an entirely different approach, saying He was the highest form of mankind, possessing a spark of divinity that He fanned into flame—a spark, they claim, we all have but seldom fan. Then there are those who believe Him to be one of many gods, a created being, a high angel, or a prophet.

The common thread of those countless human explanations is that they make Jesus less than God. Only God can tell us who He really was—and is. The biblical evidence contained in two passages—one written by the apostle Paul to a group of believers in Colossae (Col. 1:15-19), the other written by an unknown author to Jewish believers and unbelievers (Heb. 1:1-3)—offers us an overwhelming picture of the deity of Christ. Taken together, they leave no doubt that the man named Jesus, born of a virgin, was the incarnation of God, and thus is worthy of our love and devotion.

Both the apostle Paul and the writer of Hebrews had specific goals in mind in declaring the deity of Christ. In the church at Colossae, Paul had to counteract the influence of what came to be known as *gnosticism*. Its adherents fancied themselves as having privileged access to some elevated mysteries, which they believed were truths so complex that common people couldn't understand them. They taught a form of philosophic dualism, postulating that spirit was good and matter was evil. They believed that because God is spirit, He is good, but that He could never touch matter, which is evil.

Therefore, they also concluded that God couldn't be the creator of the physical universe, because if God made matter, He would be responsible for evil. And they taught that God could never become a man, because as a man He would have to dwell in a body made of evil matter. So they explained away the Incarnation by claiming that Jesus was a good angel whose body was only an illusion. But the apostle Paul says:

> He is the image of the invisible God, the firstborn of all creation. For by Him all things were created, both in the heavens and on earth, visible and invisible, whether thrones or dominions or rulers or authorities—all things have been created through Him and for Him. He is before all things, and in Him all things hold together. He is also head of the body, the church; and He is the beginning, the firstborn from the dead, so that He Himself will come to have first place in everything. For it was the Father's good pleasure for all the fullness to dwell in Him (Col. 1:15-19).

That specifically affirms Jesus as God in the flesh—the Creator of everything.

The writer of Hebrews, in contrast, was writing to Jews, some of whom did not believe Jesus to be the Messiah. In addition to affirming to Jewish believers the deity of Christ, he was trying to convince the unbelievers among them of Christ's superiority—His preeminence over any Old Testament person, institution, ritual or sacrifice. The first three verses of chapter 1 are a summary of his entire epistle, weaving into a few brief words the superiority of Christ:

> God, after He spoke long ago to the fathers in the prophets in many portions and in many ways, in these last days has spoken to us in His Son, whom He appointed heir of all things, through whom also He made the world. And He is the radiance of His glory and the exact representation of His nature, and upholds all things by the word of His power (Heb. 1:1-3).

Jesus was no mere man. Those two passages declare that He was and is the preeminent One—the climax of God's revelation. Jesus Christ is the full representation of and the human expression of God—superior to and exalted above anyone or anything. If we are ever to return to our first love, we must base our relationship with Him on that irrefutable fact. But before we can build our relationship with Him, we must see Christ in His relationship to things bigger than us. The apostle Paul and the author of Hebrews do just that. Let's examine what they have to say about our beloved and exalted Christ.

Christ and the Father

Like Father Like Son

Those who dispute the deity of Christ sometimes attempt to use Colossians 1:15-19 to support their view. They suggest, for example, that the phrase "the image of the invisible God" (v. 15) indicates that Jesus was merely a created being who bore the image of God in the same sense as all humanity. But the Greek word translated "image" here is *eikon,* which refers to a perfect replica, a precise copy, or an exact reproduction, as in a fine sculpture or portrait. Paul was saying that God Himself is fully manifest in the Person of His Son, who is none other than Jesus Christ. He is the *exact* image of God.

Hebrews 1:3 makes an identical affirmation: "He is the radiance of His glory and the exact representation of His nature." Christ is to God as the warm brilliance of light is to the sun. Just as the sun is never without its brightness, so it is with Christ and God. They cannot be divided, and neither has ever existed without the other. They are One (see John 10:30).

The Greek word translated "radiance" (*apaugasma,* "to send forth light") represents Jesus as the manifestation of God. Since no one can see God at any time (see John 1:18), and none of us ever will, the only radiance that reaches us from God is mediated to us from Jesus Christ.

We live in a world full of injustice, failure, privation, separation, disease and death. A moral darkness covers men and women, who are blinded by their godless appetites and passions. The apostle Paul confirms this fact: "Even if our gospel is veiled, it is veiled to those who are perishing, in whose case the god of this world has blinded the minds of the unbelieving so that they might not see the light of the gospel of the glory of Christ, who is the image of God" (2 Cor. 4:3-4).

But if you are Christian, God has opened your eyes to the light: "For God, who said, 'Light shall shine out of darkness,' is the One who has shone in our hearts to give the Light of the knowledge of the glory of God in the face of Christ" (v. 6). Jesus Himself said, "I am the Light of the world; he who follows Me will not walk in the darkness, but will have the Light of life" (John 8:12). We would never be able to see or enjoy God's light if we couldn't see Jesus. His light is life itself—true spiritual life, which gives us purpose, meaning, peace, joy and fellowship for all eternity.

Hebrews 1:3 also says that Christ is "the exact representation of [God's] nature." Jesus is the express image of God not only in His manifestation, but also in His very essence or substance. Even in His incarnation He set aside the use of His attributes, not the attributes themselves, so He was always fully God. "He who has seen Me," He told the disciples, "has seen the Father" (John 14:9). Paul confirmed that the glory of God shines in Jesus Christ (see 2 Cor. 4:4,6).

"Exact representation" translates the Greek word *charakter*, from which we derive the English words "character" and "characteristic." The Greeks typically used this term for an impression made by a die or stamp on a seal, in which the design on the die is reproduced on the wax. By using such terminology, the writer of Hebrews was claiming that Jesus Christ is the reproduction of God—the perfect, personal imprint of God in time and space.

Through Christ the invisible God has been made visible. God's full likeness is revealed in Him. Colossians 1:19 takes the truth a step further: "It was the Father's good pleasure for all the fullness to dwell in Him." He is not just an outline of God; He is fully God. Colossians 2:9 is even more explicit: "In Him all the fullness of Deity dwells in bodily form." Nothing is lacking. No attribute is absent. He is God in the fullest possible sense.

The Rightful Heir

In Colossians 1:15 Paul says Jesus is "the firstborn of all creation." Those who reject the deity of Christ have made much of that phrase, assuming it means Jesus was a created being and thus He could not be the eternal God. But the word translated "firstborn" (*prototokos*) describes Jesus' rank, not His origin. Although *prototokos* can mean firstborn chronologically (see Luke 2:7), it refers primarily to position. In both Greek and Jewish culture, the firstborn was the son who ranked first, and thus had the right of inheritance. As a result, the firstborn son in a royal family had the right to rule. Christ is the One who inherits all creation and the right to rule over it.

In Psalm 89:27 God says of David, "I also shall make [you] My firstborn, the highest of the kings of the earth." There the meaning of "firstborn" is given in plain language: "the highest of the kings of the earth." That's what *prototokos* means with regard to Christ— He is "Lord of lords and King of kings" (Rev. 17:14).

Hebrews 1 again offers a parallel statement: verse 2 says God has appointed His son "heir of all things." As the Son of God, Jesus is the heir of all that God possesses. Everything that exists in the universe will find its true meaning only when it comes under His control. We see that theme in the book of Psalms, where the Father says to the Son, "Ask of Me, and I will surely give the nations as Your inheritance, and the very ends of the earth as Your possession" (2:8).

In the last days, God's kingdom will be given finally and eternally to Jesus Christ (see Rev. 11:15). Revelation 5 pictures God in heaven sitting on a throne holding a sealed scroll in His hand. That scroll is the title deed to the earth and all that's in it. And He is holding it for the Heir—the One who has the right to possess the earth.

Roman law required that a will be sealed seven times to protect it from being tampered with, and that was true of this title deed. At first no one was found worthy to break its seals. But Jesus Christ, the worthy Lamb, came and took the scroll from the right hand of God because He—and He alone—had the right to do so.

Revelation 6 records the first step in Christ's taking back the earth that is rightfully His. One by one He unrolls the seals. As He breaks each seal, He takes further possession and control of His inheritance. Finally when He unrolls the seventh seal, the seventh trumpet blows, and the seventh bowl is poured out, the earth is His.

When Christ first came to earth, He became poor so that we through His poverty might be made rich (see 2 Cor. 8:9). He had nothing for Himself, "nowhere to lay His head" (Luke 9:58). Even His clothes were taken from Him when He died, and He was buried in a borrowed grave. But when Christ comes again, things will be different. He will completely and eternally inherit all things.

Those who trust their lives to Him will be fellow heirs with Him (see Rom. 8:16-17). When we enter His eternal kingdom, we will jointly possess all that He possesses. We will not be joint Christs or Lords, but we will be joint heirs of His marvelous inheritance.

Since Jesus Christ is the image of God, has the right to rule the earth, and one day will make us joint heirs of His inheritance, we owe Him our undying love and devotion. Those truths alone ought to make us return to our first love.

Christ and Creation

He Is the Creator

Colossians 1:16-17 explicitly names Christ as Creator of everything: "For by Him all things were created, both in the heavens and on earth, visible and invisible, whether thrones or dominions or rulers or authorities—all things have been created through Him and for Him. He is before all things." He is not part of creation; He is the Creator, the very arm of God, active from the beginning in calling the universe and all creatures into existence. John 1:3 says, "All things came into being through Him, and apart from Him nothing came into being that has come into being." That could not be true if He were Himself a created being.

Hebrews 1:2 also identifies Christ as the Creator. He is the Person of the Trinity through whom the world was made, the agent "through whom also [God] made the world," and for whom it was fashioned. One of the greatest proofs of Jesus' divinity is His power to create, an ability that belongs to God alone. He created everything material and everything spiritual.

Though man has stained His work with sin, Christ originally made it good, and the very creation itself longs to be restored to what it was in the beginning (see Rom. 8:21-22).

The Greek word translated "world" in Hebrews 1:2 (*aionas*) is better translated "ages." Jesus Christ is responsible for creating not only the physical earth, but also time, space, force, action and matter. Without energy or effort, He created the entire universe and everything that makes it function.

Think of what that means. The expanse of creation is staggering. Have you ever reflected on the size of the universe? If it doesn't impress on you the majesty of God, you haven't really considered it.

A ray of light travels 186,000 miles per second, so a beam of light from here will reach the moon in a second and a half. Imagine traveling that fast. You could reach Mercury in four-and-a-half minutes, Jupiter in 35 minutes. If you decided to go farther, you could reach Saturn in about an hour, but it would take four years and four months to make it to the nearest star. Traveling just to the edge of

our galaxy, the Milky Way, would take you about 100,000 years. If
you could count the stars as you travel, they would number about
100 billion in the Milky Way alone. If you wanted to explore other
galaxies, you would have billions to choose from. The size of our
universe is understandably incomprehensible.

What about life on the earth? Where did it come from? Sir John
Eccles, a Nobel laureate in neurophysiology, said in an address en-
titled "Evolution and the Conscious Self" that the odds of intelligent life evolving on earth are extremely unlikely. Amazingly, he went
on to say he believed that such did occur but could never happen
again on any other planet or in any other solar system! His strange
logic illustrates the dilemma of humanistic science: If you refuse to
recognize a Creator, it's difficult to explain how this marvelous, in-
tricate, immeasurable universe came into being.

Where did it all come from? Who conceived it? Who made it?
It can't be an accident. Someone had to make it, and the Bible tells
us its maker is Jesus Christ.

He Is the Preexistent One

Jesus holds primacy over the creation because "He is before all
things" (Col. 1:17). When the universe began, He already existed
(see John 1:1-2; 1 John 1:1). He told the Jews in John 8:58, "Before
Abraham was born, I am." He identified Himself as Yahweh, the
eternally existing God. The prophet Micah said of Him, "His go-
ings forth are from long ago, from the days of eternity" (Mic. 5:2).
Anyone existing before time began at the creation is eternal, and
only God is eternal.

He Is the Sustainer

Furthermore, Paul adds that "in Him all things hold together"
(Col. 1:17). The author of Hebrews confirms Paul's declaration:
Christ "upholds all things by the word of His power" (1:3). The
Greek word translated "upholds" means "to support or maintain."
It's used here in the present tense, implying continuous action.
Everything in the universe is being sustained right now by Jesus
Christ. He maintains the delicate balance necessary to life's exis-

tence by quite literally holding all things together. He keeps all the entities in space in motion. He is the power behind every consistency in the universe.

Can you imagine what would happen if Christ relinquished His sustaining power over the laws of the universe? If just one of the physical laws varied, we could not exist. If He suspended the law of gravity for only a brief moment, we would all perish in unimaginable ways. Consider the resulting destruction if the earth's rotation slowed just a little, or if it moved any closer or farther from the sun.

Our globe is tilted on an exact angle of 23 degrees, providing us with four seasons. If it were not so tilted, vapors from the ocean would move north and south and develop into monstrous continents of ice. If the moon didn't retain its exact distance from the earth, ocean tides would inundate the land. If the ocean floors were merely a few feet deeper than they are, the carbon dioxide and oxygen balance of the earth's atmosphere would be completely upset, and no animal or plant life could exist. If the atmosphere's density thinned even a little, many of the meteors that now harmlessly burn up when they hit the atmosphere would constantly bombard the earth's surface.

How does our world maintain such a fantastically delicate balance? Through Jesus Christ, who sustains and monitors all its movements. He is the very principle of cohesion. Don't buy the lie of deism, which says that God made everything, wound it up like a watch, and has not bothered with it since. The universe is a cosmos, not a chaos—an ordered, reliable system instead of an erratic, unpredictable muddle—only because Jesus Christ upholds it all. Knowing that, how could any Christian not bow before Him to love and adore Him?

Christ and the Unseen World

Christ also has a particular relationship with the unseen spiritual realm, since He is the creator of "thrones," "dominions," "rulers" and "authorities" (Col. 1:16). Those terms refer to the various ranks of angels Christ created. The writer of Hebrews also makes a clear distinction between Christ and the angels: "Of the angels He says, 'Who makes His angels winds, and His ministers a flame of fire.' But of the Son He says, 'Your throne, O God, is forever and ever, and the righteous scepter is the scepter of His kingdom'" (Heb. 1:7-8).

Scripture is clear that Jesus is not an angel, but the Creator of the angels. He is above the angels, who in fact worship Him and are under His authority. Jesus' relation to the unseen world, like His relation to the visible universe, proves He is God.

Christ and the Church

Paul concludes his treatise on the preeminence of Christ with four great realities about His relationship to the church: "He is also head of the body, the church; and He is the beginning, the first-born from the dead; so that He Himself will come to have first place in everything" (Col. 1:18).

He Is the Head

Scripture uses many metaphors to describe the church, but none so graphic as that of a human body. The church is a body, and that means Christ is the Head of the body. The church is not merely an organization; it is a living organism, controlled by the living Christ. He rules every part of it and gives it life and direction. Because He lives His life through all the members, He produces unity in the body (see 1 Cor. 12:12-20). He energizes and coordinates diversity within the body, a diversity manifested in spiritual gifts and ministries (see vv. 4-13). He also directs the body's mutuality, as the individual members serve and support each other (see vv. 15-27).

He Is the Source

Christ is also the "beginning" of the church. *Arche* ("beginning") refers to source, rank or primacy. It can be translated "chief" or "pioneer." Since Christ is both the source of the church and its chief, the church has its origins in Him. God "chose us in Him before the foundation of the world" (Eph. 1:4). As Head of the body, Jesus holds the chief position, or highest rank, in the church. As the beginning of it, He is its originator.

He Is the Firstborn from the Dead
Earlier in this chapter we discussed the meaning of "firstborn." Of all those who have been raised from the dead, or ever will be, Christ is the highest in rank. He is the greatest One of all.

He Is the Preeminent One
Much is made of acquiring first place in our day. From sports to business, the goal of teams and corporations is to be number one. But there is only One who truly holds first place. As a result of His death and resurrection, Jesus has first place in everything. It stands to reason that the One who is first in rank in the universe has the right to that position.

Paul sums up his argument: "For it was the Father's good pleasure for all the fullness to dwell in Him" (Col. 1:19). *Pleroma* ("fullness") was a term used by the later Gnostics to refer to the divine powers and attributes, which they believed were divided among various emanations. Paul's point is that all the fullness of deity is not spread out in small doses to a group of spirits, but fully dwells in Christ alone (see 2:9). The Colossians did not need angels to help them get saved; in Christ, and in Him alone, they were complete (see v. 10). Christians share in His fullness: "For of His fullness we have all received, and grace upon grace" (John 1:16). All the fullness of Christ becomes available to those who place their trust in Him.

What should our response be to these glorious truths? The Puritan John Owen astutely observed:

> The revelation made of Christ in the blessed gospel is far more excellent, more glorious, more filled with rays of

divine wisdom and goodness than the whole creation, and the just comprehension of it, if attainable, can contain or afford. Without this knowledge, the mind of man, however priding itself in other inventions and discoveries, is wrapped up in darkness and confusion.

This therefore deserves the severest of our thoughts, the best of our meditations, and our utmost diligence in them. For if our future blessedness shall consist in living where He is, and beholding of His glory, what better preparation can there be for it than a constant previous contemplation of that glory as revealed in the gospel, that by a view of it we may be gradually transformed into the same glory?[1]

God says His Son has first place in all things. What does that mean to you? It ought to mean everything. To reject Him is to be shut out of His presence into an eternal hell. But to receive Him is to enter into all that He is and has—there are no other choices.

If you are to ever regain your first love, it is absolutely necessary for you to acknowledge that Jesus does in fact have first place in everything, including your life. You do not occupy a position of prominence, only He does. The sooner you recognize that the quicker you will begin to reestablish your love for Him.

Note
1. John Owen, *The Glory of Christ* (Chicago: Moody Press, 1949), pp. 25-26.

GOD'S GLORIOUS PLAN

How can I know God? You don't hear that question asked too often in our society. You are, however, more likely to hear questions like: *Am I valuable? Can I find a way to accept myself as I am?* And you'll find numerous opinions suggesting answers to those questions.

Our society propagates books and seminars addressing the themes of psychology, self-image and self-worth that present non-biblical techniques to help people rid themselves of guilt, fear and inadequacy. But no one can develop a true sense of personal fulfillment by playing psychological games of boosting pride. Such an emphasis is not unlike what the Pharisees did. They extolled external acts while ignoring spiritual realities (see Matt. 23). Although that kind of effort may establish a *feeling* of self-worth, there will be no change in the soul. Instead, guilt, fear, anxiety and depression are submerged in an effort to hide from the truth.

The plain fact is that man is morally and spiritually bankrupt. Nothing he can do will ever produce righteousness or give him value. Romans 3:10-12 gives us the reason: "There is none righteous, not even one; there is none who understands, there is none who seeks for God; all have turned aside, together they have become useless; there is none who does good, there is not even one." All efforts at establishing self-righteousness are doomed to fail because man on his own is incapable of doing good.

Genuine meaning and purpose can only come out of a right relationship to the Creator. Notice that we are dependent on God establishing the relationship since "there is none who seeks for God" (v. 11). Man, left to his own devices, manufactures religions and gods of his own choosing, which have nothing to do with the true God. A person without Christ has no spiritual value, no standing before God, and no meaning or purpose in the world. He is like "chaff which the wind drives away" (Ps. 1:4).

A Christian, however, is a child of God and a joint heir with Christ, having been chosen in Christ before the foundation of the world (see Eph. 1:4). The record of God's redemptive history is that of His reaching down and drawing to Himself those whom He has chosen to save. As Christians we have significance to fulfill the divine purpose only by knowing God and His Son, realizing that apart from any inherent value in us, and out of grace and in divine sovereignty, He chose each one of us to belong to Him.

God picked the nation of Israel as His chosen people purely on His own uninfluenced initiative. While they were still wandering in the desert of Sinai, Moses said:

> The Lord did not set His love on you nor choose you because you were more in number than any of the peoples, for you were the fewest of all peoples, but because the Lord loved you and kept the oath which He swore to your forefathers, the Lord brought you out by a mighty hand and redeemed you from the house of slavery, from the hand of Pharaoh king of Egypt (Deut. 7:7-8).

God did not choose them based on some inherent value or achievement, but on His love for them and His desire for them to fulfill His purpose.

The same is true of God's choosing believers. His choice is based solely on His divine will and purpose. The apostle John wrote of Jesus, "But as many as received Him, to them He gave the right to become children of God, even to those who believe in His name, who were born, not of blood nor of the will of the flesh nor of the will of man, but of God" (John 1:12-13). There is no greater value than realizing that you were specially chosen by God to be a part of His family. Nothing can compare to that. So why do so many Christians turn their backs on God and leave their first love for some unfulfilling worldly pursuit? An understanding of God's marvelous plan of salvation and all that He has for you as a member of His family will go a long way in helping you regain your first love.

Ephesians 1:3-6 is a record of God's role in our salvation and what He has made available to us through His Son. These verses take us back to eternity past, letting us eavesdrop on God's plan to save us—not only long before we were born but also before the earth was born. Paul writes:

> Blessed be the God and Father of our Lord Jesus Christ, who has blessed us with every spiritual blessing in the heavenly places in Christ, just as He chose us in Him before the foundation of the world, that we would be holy and blameless before Him. In love He predestined us to adoption as sons through Jesus Christ to Himself, according to the kind intention of His will, to the praise of the glory of His grace.

While God is the focus of those verses, you need to understand the role Christ has in carrying out God's salvation plan. It is through our union with Him that we receive salvation and the blessings of God.

The Agency of Christ

You are no doubt familiar with the function of an agent. The dictionary defines an agent as "one empowered to act for or represent another." Some of the most powerful people in the entertainment and sports industries are the high-priced agents who represent famous celebrities or athletes. You're probably more familiar with lower-profile agents, such as an insurance agent who represents the insured and the insurance company, or a real estate agent who represents a buyer and seller.

In a similar fashion, Christ is God's agent when it comes to salvation. Notice these phrases from Ephesians 1: we have been blessed "with every spiritual blessing in the heavenly places *in* Christ" (v. 3), "He chose us *in* Him" (v. 4), and "He predestined us to adoption as sons *through* Jesus Christ to Himself" (v. 5, emphasis added in each case).

When we trust in Christ as our Lord and Savior, we are placed into a marvelous union with Him. First Corinthians 6:17 says, "The one who joins himself to the Lord is one spirit with him." Our unity with Christ is more than simply common agreement—it is the deep, internal commonness of sharing eternal life with God.

Romans 8:16-17 says, "We are children of God, and if children, heirs also, heirs of God and fellow-heirs with Christ." When we came to know Jesus Christ, we became fellow-heirs with Him, and God dispensed to us all His riches through Him. Because we are one in Jesus Christ, His righteousness is imputed to us and His inheritance is ours. His position is now our position, His privilege is now our privilege, His possessions are now our possessions, and His practice is now our practice. We are significant not because of who we are, but because of what we become in Christ.

Our relationship to Christ takes on added significance when we realize that we are a gift from God to His Son. Christ understood that when He said to the Father, "I have manifested Your name to the men whom You gave Me out of the world; they were Yours and You gave them to Me, and they have kept Your word" (John 17:6). Regarding this topic D. Martyn Lloyd-Jones writes:

> These people . . . belonged to God before they became the Son's people. Our position does not depend upon anything we do, primarily; nor primarily even upon the action of the Son. The primary action is that of God the Father who chose unto Himself a people out of the whole of mankind before the foundation of the world, and then presented, gave these people whom He had chosen to the Son, in order that the Son might redeem them and do everything that was necessary for their reconciliation with Himself. That is the teaching of the Lord Jesus Christ Himself. He came into the world, and accomplished His

work, for these people who have been given to Him by the Father. . . . But it is of vital importance that we should re-member that it is all done "in Him." The apostle continu-ally repeats the truth that there is nothing whatsoever given to the Christian apart from the Lord Jesus Christ; there is no relationship to God which is true and saving except that which is in and through the Son of God. "There is one God, and one mediator [only] between God and men, the man Christ Jesus" (1 Timothy 2:5).[1]

We can only scratch the surface of the depth of the relation-ship between the Father and the Son revealed in John 17. The gift God promised (see 2 Tim. 1:9; Titus 1:2) to give the Son was a re-deemed humanity that would ultimately glorify Him for what He had done. Romans 8:29 reveals how that works out in God's ulti-mate purpose for our salvation: "Whom He foreknew, He also pre-destined to become conformed to the image of His Son, so that He would be the firstborn among many brethren."

From before time began, God chose to save believers from their sins that they might "become conformed to the image of His Son," Jesus Christ. Consequently, every true believer moves inex-orably toward perfection in righteousness, as God makes for Him-self a people re-created in the likeness of His own divine Son (see Gal. 4:19; Col. 1:28; 1 John 3:2), who will dwell and reign with Him in heaven throughout all eternity. God is redeeming for Himself an eternally holy and Christlike race, to be citizens in His divine kingdom and children in His divine family.

Ultimately though, God's supreme purpose for bringing sin-ners to salvation is to glorify His Son, Jesus Christ, by making Him preeminent in the divine plan of redemption. It is God's intent for Christ to "be the firstborn among many brethren" (Rom. 8:29). As we noted in the first chapter, "firstborn" was often used in Jewish culture figuratively to represent preeminence. That is its meaning in the present context.

As it is in almost every instance in the New Testament, the term "brethren" is synonymous for "believers." God's primary purpose in His plan of redemption was to make His beloved Son "the first-born among many brethren" in the sense of Christ's being uniquely preeminent among the children of God. Those who trust in Him become God's adopted children, and Jesus, the Son of God, graciously calls them His brothers and sisters in God's divine family (see Matt. 12:50). God's purpose is to make us like Christ to create a great redeemed and glorified humanity over which He will reign and be forever preeminent. Thus our ultimate purpose as the redeemed children of God will be to spend eternity worshiping and giving praise to God's beloved "firstborn," our preeminent Lord and Savior, Jesus Christ. Paul referred to that purpose as "the prize of the upward call of God" (Phil. 3:14), meaning the reward of heaven. That was "the goal" Paul strived for in this life, and it certainly ought to be the focus of those who would return to their first love.

The Blessings of Our Salvation

Having seen Christ's role with respect to God's plan of salvation, let's turn to Paul's discussion of what God the Father planned for His children. Paul begins in Ephesians 1 by informing His readers and us of the tremendous blessings available to those who are saved.

The Blessed One

Paul starts by praising the One who has provided the blessing: "Blessed be the God and Father of our Lord Jesus Christ" (v. 3). The Greek word translated "blessed" is *eulogetos,* from which we derive the English word "eulogy." It is a declaration of an individual's goodness.

The Bible records the goodness of God from beginning to end. Melchizedek declared, "Blessed be God Most High" (Gen. 14:20). In the last days "every created thing which is in heaven and on the earth and under the earth and on the sea, and all things in them" will be "heard saying, 'To Him who sits on the throne, and to the Lamb, be blessing and honor and glory and dominion forever and ever'" (Rev. 5:13).

Consistent with His perfection and praiseworthiness, the One who is to be supremely blessed for His goodness is Himself the One "who has blessed us." James says that "every good thing given and every perfect gift is from above, coming down from the Father of lights, with whom there is no variation or shifting shadow" (1:17). Romans 8:28 says, "God causes all things to work together for good to those who love God, to those who are called according to His purpose." God is good and blesses because He is the source of every good thing.

The Blessed Ones

The recipients of God's blessing are believers. In His marvelous providence, wonderful grace, and sovereign plan, God has chosen to be eternally good to us. When we praise His goodness, we bless Him. When He blesses us, He communicates good to us. We bless Him with words; He blesses us with deeds. Our heavenly Father lavishes us with every good gift. That is His nature, and that is our need.

The Blessings

Paul next tells us that we have been blessed "with all spiritual blessings." Unfortunately, most believers are unaware of the extent of those blessings and are constantly asking God for things He has already provided. They pray for such things as love, peace, joy and strength, when all the while those very blessings are theirs for the taking (e.g., Rom. 5:5; John 14:27; 15:11; Phil. 4:13). God has given us all spiritual blessings, yet we need to ask for wisdom in understanding how to use those resources (see Jas. 1:5).

There are no missing ingredients in God's blessing. It is not that God *will* give us, but that He has *already* given us "everything pertaining to life and godliness" (2 Pet. 1:3). He has blessed us already with every spiritual blessing. Our resources in Christ are not simply promised to us; they are actually in our possession. Every believer has what Paul calls "the provision of the Spirit of Jesus Christ" (Phil. 1:19). God cannot give us more than He has already given us in Christ—we are complete in Him (see Col. 2:10). The believer's need, therefore, is not to receive something more but to do something more with what he has.

The Location of Blessing

Our abundant, unlimited resources and realities reside "in the heavenly places," an area that encompasses the entire supernatural realm of God. While it includes heaven, it's not limited to that. It refers to all things that are transcendent, eternal and spiritual—love, forgiveness, peace—all those elements that reside only in the kingdom of God. This is no promise of health, wealth and success in this world. Just the opposite, it is the promise of things not of this world.

Christians are not so much citizens of the earth as they are citizens of heaven. Philippians 3:20 says plainly, "Our citizenship is in heaven, from which also we eagerly wait for a Savior, the Lord Jesus Christ." Because we are citizens of heaven, we are able to understand the supernatural things of God, things that the "natural man does not accept" and "cannot understand . . . because they are spiritually appraised" (1 Cor. 2:14).

When an American citizen travels abroad, he remains as much an American citizen as when he is in the United States. Whether he is in Africa, the Near East, Europe, or anywhere outside his homeland, he is still an American citizen and possesses all the rights and privileges that accompany his citizenship.

As citizens of God's heavenly kingdom, Christians possess all the rights and privileges that citizenship grants (some present, some future), even while they are living in the "foreign" and hostile environment of earth. Our true life is in heaven—our Father, Savior, family, loved ones and home are there. While there is much we long for in heaven, we must continue our sojourn on earth for as long as the Lord wills.

The key to living as a heavenly citizen while living in this world is to walk by the Spirit (see Gal. 5:16). In so doing, Paul says, "you will not carry out the desire of the flesh." Instead, we will be the beneficiaries of the fruit of the Spirit (see vv. 22-23). We receive our blessings by living in the power of the Spirit.

If you are ever tempted to let earthly pursuits become the priority in your life, remember the abundance of blessings God has for you. Then you'll be sure to hang on to your first love.

The Plan of Salvation

Some of God's ways we will never understand as fully as others, for "the secret things belong to the Lord" (Deut. 29:29). Isaiah 55:9 tells us that God's ways are higher than man's ways. And that is certainly true when it comes to the doctrine of election. In Ephesians 1:4-6 Paul writes, "He chose us in Him before the foundation of the world, that we should be holy and blameless before Him. In love He predestined us to adoption as sons through Jesus Christ to Himself, according to the kind intention of His will, to the praise of the glory of His grace." Those verses reveal the past aspect of God's eternal plan of salvation.

The Method: Sovereign Election

The Bible teaches three kinds of election. One is God's theocratic election of Israel (see Deut. 7:6). But that had no bearing on personal salvation. Racial descent from Abraham as father of the Hebrew people did not mean spiritual descent from him as father of the faithful (see Rom. 4:11).

A second kind of election is vocational. The Lord called out the tribe of Levi to be His priests, but they were not guaranteed salvation. Jesus chose twelve men as apostles, yet Judas was not a believer.

The third kind of election is salvational, the type Paul is referring to in Ephesians 1:4. Jesus explained, "No one can come to Me unless the Father who sent Me draws him" (John 6:44). No one is saved unless he is drawn (Greek *helkuo*). That term is used in nonbiblical writings to speak of an irresistible force. For example, it is used of a hungry man being drawn to food and of the power of love that draws two people together. This drawing force of God can be likened to an electromagnet that draws iron while leaving nonferrous metal unmoved. God's election is irresistible to those upon whom He has set His love. The elect will respond in faith to the divine magnet.

Completely apart from any merit of any individual, God chose us in Christ. By God's sovereign election, those who are saved were placed in eternal union with Christ Jesus before creation even took place.

Although man's will is not free in the sense that many people suppose, it is still part of his being. Apart from God, that will is captive to sin. But he still has the capacity and responsibility to choose God because God makes that choice possible. And God has to do it, because if left to our own abilities, we could never choose Him (see Rom. 3:11).

Jesus said that whoever believes in Him will not perish but have eternal life (see John 3:16) and that "everyone who lives and believes in Me will never die" (11:26). The frequent commands to the unsaved to respond to the Lord (e.g., Matt. 3:1-2; 4:17; John 11:28-30) clearly indicate the responsibility of man to exercise his own will. Yet the Bible is just as clear that no person receives Jesus Christ as Savior and Lord who has not been chosen by God (see Rom. 8:29; 1 Pet. 1:2). Jesus gives both truths in one verse in the Gospel of John: "All that the Father gives Me will come to Me; and the one who comes to Me I will certainly not cast out" (John 6:37).

God's sovereign election and man's exercise of responsibility in choosing Jesus Christ seem opposite and irreconcilable truths. In his book *Evangelism and the Sovereignty of God*, J.I. Packer warns of the dangers of attempting to reconcile them:

> People see the Bible teaches man's responsibility for his actions; they do not see . . . how this is consistent with the sovereign Lordship of God over those actions. They are not content to let the two truths live side by side, as they do in the Scriptures, but jump to the conclusion that, in order to uphold the biblical truth of human responsibility, they are bound to reject the equally biblical and equally true doctrine of divine sovereignty, and to explain away the great number of texts that teach it. The desire to over-

simplify the Bible by cutting out the mysteries is natural to our perverse minds, and it is not surprising that even good men should fall victim to it. Hence this persistent and troublesome dispute. The irony of the situation, however, is that when we ask how the two sides pray, it becomes apparent that those who profess to deny God's sovereignty really believe in it just as strongly as those who affirm it.[2]

Divine sovereignty and human responsibility are integral and inseparable realities of salvation—though exactly how they operate together only the infinite mind of God knows.

The Time: Eternity Past

God elected us "before the foundation of the world." Before the creation of the universe we were sovereignly predestined by God to be His. The apostle Peter declared that we were redeemed "with precious blood, as of a lamb unblemished and spotless, the blood of Christ. For He was foreknown before the foundation of the world" (1 Pet. 1:19-20). Just as Christ's crucifixion was planned out before the world began, so we were designated for salvation by that same plan at that same time. It was then that our inheritance in God's kingdom was determined (see Matt. 25:34). We belonged to God before time began, and we will be His after time has run its course. Our names were "written from the foundation of the world in the book of life of the Lamb who has been slain" (Rev. 13:8).

The Purpose: Holiness/Christlikeness

We noted earlier the purpose of God's plan of salvation regarding Christ, but what was His purpose with respect to those He saved? Paul says that it was so that we might be "holy and blameless" (Eph. 1:4). The Greek word translated "blameless" (*amomos*) literally means "without blemish" or "spotless." Paul also said we were "predestined to become conformed to the image of His Son" (Rom. 8:29).

Because Christ gave Himself for us as "a lamb unblemished and spotless" (1 Pet. 1:19), God has given us His own unblemished and spotless nature. The unworthy have been declared worthy, the unrighteous declared holy.

Obviously that is our position in Christ, but our practice is far from Christlike and far from blameless. Yet in Colossians 2:10 Paul says, "In Him [we] have been made complete." All that God is we become in Jesus Christ. That's why our salvation is secure—we have Christ's perfect righteousness. Our practice can and does fall short, but our position can never fall short, because it is the same holy and blameless position Christ has before God. We are as secure as our Savior because we are in Him. And because God has declared us to be holy and blameless, we should strive to reflect that in our lives by pursuing the very image of Christ (see Phil. 3:9-14) as we live in this world. You'll never leave your first love as long as Christ is the passion and priority in your life.

The Motive: Love

God chose us to be His children because of His love (see John 3:16). Biblical *agape* love is not an emotion; it is an act of self-sacrifice on behalf of others. The preeminent expression of God's love is the death of His Son: "Greater love has no one than this, that one lay down his life for his friends" (John 15:13).

That is exactly what Jesus Himself did on behalf of those whom God chose to save. In the ultimate divine act of love, God determined before the foundation of the earth that He would give His only Son to save us. Paul says, "God, being rich in mercy, because of His great love with which He loved us, even when we were dead in our transgressions, made us alive together with Christ" (Eph. 2:4-5).

The Result: Sonship

The result of God's election is that "He predestined us to adoption as sons through Jesus Christ to Himself" (Eph. 1:5). In Christ we became subjects of His kingdom, and because He is our Lord we are His servants. He even calls us friends (see John 15:15). But in His great love He makes us more than citizens and servants, and even more than friends—He makes us children, lovingly drawing us into the intimacy of His own family.

We became His children the instant we were saved (see John 1:12). In fact, as His children, we can now address God in an intimate way—"Abba," the Aramaic equivalent of "Daddy" (Gal. 4:6). Our adoption means that the life of God dwells in us. Human parents can adopt children and love them as much as they do their natural children. But no human parent can impart his or her distinct nature to an adopted child. Yet that is exactly what God has done for us. We actually are "partakers of the divine nature" (2 Pet. 1:4) in that the Spirit of God dwells in us (see Gal. 4:6).

The Reason: Glory

Why did God do all this for us? Paul says it is "according to the kind intention of His will, to the praise of the glory of His grace" (Eph. 1:5-6). Above all else, He elects and saves us for His own glory. When Jesus told His disciples, "Your Father has chosen gladly to give you the kingdom" (Luke 12:32), He was affirming the delight of God in putting His glory on display.

All creation exists to bring glory to God. In Isaiah 43:20 God says, "The beasts of the field will glorify Me." Psalm 19:1 says, "The heavens are telling of the glory of God." The only rebels in the universe are fallen angels and fallen men. Everything else glorifies its Creator. The fallen angels have already been eternally removed from God's presence, and so will the fallen men who refuse to be saved by Jesus Christ.

God chose and preordained who would be conformed to the image of Christ before the foundation of the world so that no human being could boast or take glory for himself, but that all the glory might be His. Salvation is all from God, and therefore all the glory belongs to Him. To guarantee that, every provision of salvation was designed before any human being was ever born.

The ultimate reason for everything that exists is the honor of the Almighty. That is why, as God's children, Christians should do everything they do "to the glory of God" (1 Cor. 10:31).

As you can see, our purpose comes from knowing that we are the object of God's love, and that He chose us to be members of His divine family. Since you are a child of the King, you have become precious to Him. And because God has given us all spiritual blessings in the heavenlies, we have an unlimited supply of divine resources. Be sure to use them to make your life fulfilling, to minister with the greatest amount of power, and fulfill the purpose of the church that Jesus purchased with His precious blood.

In the first chapter we have seen that Christ is God, the Creator and Sustainer of the universe, and the One who has the right to rule over it. In this chapter we have seen the role that Christ plays in God's magnificent plan of salvation. In the following chapters we will look at what Christ did to accomplish God's plan, and how that makes Him worthy of your complete and pure devotion.

Notes

1. D. Martyn Lloyd-Jones, *God's Ultimate Purpose: An Exposition of Ephesians 1:1 to 23* (Grand Rapids, MI: Baker Books, 1979), p. 94.
2. J. I Packer, *Evangelism and the Sovereignty of God* (Chicago: InterVarsity Press, 1961), pp. 16-17.

JESUS OUR SAVIOR

IN THE LIKENESS
OF MEN

British author C. S. Lewis, in the chapter "The Grand Miracle" from his book *Miracles,* described the incarnation of Christ in this manner:

> In the Christian story God descends to re-ascend. He comes down; down from the heights of absolute being into time and space, down into humanity ... down to the very roots and sea-bed of the Nature He has created.
>
> But He goes down to come up again and bring the ruined world up with Him. One has the picture of a strong man stooping lower and lower to get himself underneath some great complicated burden. He must stoop in order to lift, he must almost disappear under the load before he incredibly straightens his back and marches off with the whole mass swaying on his shoulders.
>
> Or one may think of a diver, first reducing himself to nakedness, then glancing in mid-air, then gone with a splash, vanished, rushing down through green and warm water into black and cold water, down through increasing pressure into the death-like region of ooze and slime and old decay; then up again, back to colour and light, his lungs almost bursting, till suddenly he breaks surface again, holding in his hand the dripping, precious thing that he went down to recover. He and it are both coloured now

that they have come up into the light: down below, where it lay colourless in the dark, he lost his colour, too.

In this descent and re-ascent everyone will recognise a familiar pattern: a thing written all over the world. It is the pattern of all vegetable life. It must belittle itself into something hard, small and deathlike, it must fall into the ground: thence the new life re-ascends.

It is the pattern of all animal generation too. There is descent from the full and perfect organisms into the spermatozoon and ovum, and in the dark womb a life at first inferior in kind to that of the species which is being reproduced: then the slow ascent to the perfect embryo, to the living, conscious baby, and finally to the adult.

So it is also in our moral and emotional life. The first innocent and spontaneous desires have to submit to the deathlike process of control or total denial: but from that there is a re-ascent to fully formed character in which the strength of the original material all operates but in a new way. Death and Rebirth—go down to go up—it is a key principle. Through this bottleneck, this belittlement, the highroad nearly always lies.[1]

What Lewis described so eloquently, God did for us. Jesus Christ, God's only Son, left His exalted place with God the Father, and humiliated Himself to become a man that He might carry out God's plan of salvation. Jesus Christ, the very Creator and Sustainer of the universe, condescended to become a creature so that He could save those whom God had chosen from before the foundation of the world.

Our previous chapters merely set the stage for what we are about to examine in the remainder of the book, for now we'll see God's plan in action. There's great joy and comfort not only in knowing God chose you to be saved, but also in seeing how He accomplished it. That leads us to one of the most profound passages in all Scripture: Philippians 2:5-8. Here the apostle Paul describes the incarnation of Christ—the central miracle of Christianity:

Have this attitude in yourselves which was also in Christ
Jesus, who, although He existed in the form of God, did
not regard equality with God a thing to be grasped, but
emptied Himself, taking the form of a bond-servant, and
being made in the likeness of men. Being found in appearance as a man, He humbled Himself by becoming obedient to the point of death, even death on a cross.

The Greek text hints that this passage was probably a hymn of
the early church. Theologians have called it a Christological gem—
a sparkling diamond of the New Testament because it is unparal-
leled in its analysis of the incarnation of God in Christ. Yet as
crucial as it is theologically, this passage is first and foremost eth-
ical. The context reveals that Paul was striving to motivate believers to live out their faith.

Through the inspiration of the Holy Spirit he uses the facts of
the Incarnation to offer the supreme illustration of humility—an
illustration we are called to follow. Paul's inspired description is
the supreme portrait of self-sacrifice, self-denial, self-giving, and
boundless love for God on the part of Christ.

At the same time that we survey His example of humility, you
need to see through to His love for you as well. Beyond His example of humility is what that humble act accomplished: the redemption of your soul. Renewing your love for Christ must begin at this
point. Only as you remember what He willingly gave up for you will
you dutifully follow His example and do nothing out of selfishness
or conceit, and instead regard others as more important than yourself. There is no greater way to demonstrate your love for Him.

Christ Was God

Paul began by affirming that Jesus is God when he said that He
"existed in the form of God" (Phil. 2:6). That is the point where the
Incarnation began and from which Christ began the descent of
His humiliation. The Greek word translated "existed" (*huparcho*)
stresses the essence of a person's nature—the continuous state or

condition of something.[2] It expresses what one is unalterably and inalienably in essence. Paul's point was that Jesus Christ is continuously existing without change.

The meaning of the Greek word translated "form" (*morphe*) "always signifies a form which truly and fully expresses the being which underlies it."[3] That means it describes the essential being or nature of that which it refers to, in this case the essential being of God.

Morphe is better understood when compared to the Greek word *schema*, which is also translated "form." *Morphe* expresses the essential character of something—what it is in itself—while *schema* emphasizes outward form or appearance. What *morphe* expresses never changes, while what *schema* represents can. For example, all men possess manhood from the time they are conceived until they die. That is their *morphe*. But the essential character of manhood is shown in various *schema*. At one time a man is an embryo, then a baby, then a child, then a boy, then a youth, then a young man, then an adult, and finally an old man.

By using *morphe* in Philippians 2, Paul was saying Jesus possessed the unchangeable, essential nature of God. That interpretation of the first phrase of verse 6 is strengthened by the second phrase, "He did not regard equality with God something to be grasped," which indicates Jesus was equal with God. Being in the form of God thus expresses Christ's equality to God.

The deity of Christ is the heart and soul of the Christian faith. One of the goals of the apostle John in writing his Gospel was to leave his readers with little doubt that Jesus is God. He began by saying, "In the beginning was the Word [Christ], and the Word was with God, and the Word was God. . . . All things came into being through Him, and apart from Him nothing came into being that has come into being. In Him was life, and the life was the Light of men" (John 1:1,3-4). He also said that Christ "became flesh, and dwelt among us, and we saw His glory, glory as of the only begotten from the Father" (v. 14). In the first chapter, we examined two additional passages that also affirmed the deity of Christ: Colossians 1:15-17 and Hebrews 1:3. Christianity begins with the recognition that Jesus Christ is in essence fully the eternal God.

That is also the starting point of Christ's humiliation. He descended from the exalted place of possessing the being of God. Although we cannot begin to understand the humiliation Christ experienced, we can follow His example. After all, we are the children of God, blessed with all spiritual blessings in the heavenlies in Christ (see Eph. 1:3). We have been chosen in Him (see v. 4). We are a special people who have been promised heaven's eternal glory. And we possess an exalted position as sons of God. Therefore, our humiliation begins with a recognition of the lofty starting point from which we are required to descend for the benefit of others. The simple and profound truth is that God became man and we are to be servants like Him. We are to follow the example of our first love.

Christ Did Not Cling to Equality with God

Although Jesus was equal with God, He "did not regard equality with God a thing to be grasped." The Greek word translated "equality" (*isos*) describes things exactly equal in size, quantity, quality, character and number. The English word "isomer" comes from it. Isomers are chemical molecules that vary according to structure from each other, but are identical according to atomic elements and weights. We could say their forms are different while their essential character is the same. *Isomorph* (equal form), *isometric* (equal measures), and *isosceles triangle* (a triangle with two sides of equal measure) are all English terms descriptive of equality.

The first step in Christ's humiliation was His willingness to not hold on to His equality with God. Although He did not cling to it, there is no question that Jesus claimed it and that the people who heard Him knew He claimed it. John wrote, "The Jews were seeking all the more to kill Him, because He not only was breaking the Sabbath, but also was calling God His own Father, making Himself equal with God" (John 5:18). Many today desire to deny the deity of Christ, yet even His worst enemies, the apostate religious leaders, understood full well the significance of His claim: "For a good work we do not stone You, but for blasphemy; and because You, being a man, make Yourself out to be God" (10:33).

Although He possessed all the rights, privileges and honors of being God, Christ didn't regard them as things "to be grasped." The Greek word translated "grasped" originally referred to something seized in a robbery. It eventually came to mean anything one held on to tightly. Our Lord proved that loftiness of calling is not something to be held tightly as a prized possession, to be selfishly exploited, or never set aside for the benefit of another.

The message of Christianity is far different from the world's man-made religious systems, where worshipers seek to appease the anger of their respective gods. Our God looked down on wretched sinners who hated Him and willingly yielded His privileges to give Himself for their sake. Paul said, "When the kindness of God our Savior and His love for mankind appeared, He saved us, not on the basis of deeds which we have done in righteousness, but according to His mercy, by the washing of regeneration and renewing by the Holy Spirit" (Titus 3:4-5; see also 2:11). The Incarnation expresses both the mercy and the unselfish nature of the Second Person of the Trinity.

Christ Emptied Himself

Instead of clinging to His equality with God, Christ "emptied Himself" (Phil. 2:7). The Greek verb translated "emptied" (*kenoo*) gives us the theological term *kenosis,* which is the doctrine of Christ's self-emptying (a significant aspect of His incarnation). The verb expresses His self-renunciation—His refusal to cling to His advantages and privileges as God as He descended into a humble, human state.

Yet at no time did He empty Himself of His deity in exchange for humanity. He is coexistent with the Father and the Spirit, and for Him to have become less than God would have meant the Trinity would have ceased to exist. Christ could not become less than who He truly is. He retained His divine nature while giving up the following privileges so that He could descend to the desperate level of unworthy sinners.

Heavenly Glory

Shortly before His earthly mission came to a close, Jesus prayed, "Glorify Me together with Yourself, with the glory which I had with You before the world was" (John 17:5). Christ gave up the glory of a face-to-face relationship with God for the muck of this earth. He relinquished the adoring presence of angels for the spittle of men. He sacrificed the shining brilliance of heaven's glories and emptied Himself. On a few occasions during His earthly ministry, the supernatural fullness of the glory of Christ came through, such as on the Mount of Transfiguration (see Luke 9:28-36). You can catch glimpses of Christ's glory in His miracles, attitude and words, as well as at His crucifixion, His resurrection and His ascension. But Christ emptied Himself of the continuous outward manifestation and personal enjoyment of heavenly glory.

Independent Authority

Our Lord also emptied Himself of His independent authority. He completely submitted Himself to the will of the Father and learned to be a servant. Philippians 2:8 says that He was obedient, and we see that illustrated when He said in the garden, "Not as I will, but as You will" (Matt. 26:39). "He learned obedience from the things which He suffered" (Heb. 5:8), and affirmed that He came to do His Father's will (see John 5:30)—not His own.

Divine Prerogatives

Jesus also set aside the prerogatives and expression of His divine nature, voluntarily limiting His divine attributes, though He did not cease being God. For example, He remained omniscient—He knew what was in man (see John 2:25). He was still omnipresent—though not physically present, He saw Nathanael under a tree (see 1:45-49). While He didn't give up any of His deity, He did give up the free exercise of His attributes, limiting Himself to the degree of not even knowing the time of His second coming (see Matt. 24:36).

Eternal Riches

It is impossible for us to fully understand the divine riches that belong to Christ, yet He gave it all up: "Though He was rich, yet for

[our] sake He became poor, that [we] through His poverty might become rich" (2 Cor. 8:9). Christ was so poor that He said, "The foxes have holes and the birds of the air have nests, but the Son of Man has nowhere to lay His head" (Matt. 8:20).

A Favorable Relationship

God "made Him who knew no sin to be sin on our behalf" (2 Cor. 5:21). As a result, Jesus cried out on the cross, "My God, My God, why have You forsaken Me?" (Matt. 27:46); He experienced alienation from the triune God of whom He was part. As He anticipated the completion of His work, He asked the Father to restore that preincarnate glory and relationship (see John 17:4-5).

Christ Became a Servant

When Christ emptied Himself, He not only gave up His privileges, but He also took "the form of a bond-servant" (Phil. 2:7). Paul again used *morphe* to indicate that Christ took on the essential character of a servant. His servitude was not theatrical or make-believe. He didn't just put on the garment of a slave—He actually became one.

As God, Christ owns everything. But when He came into this world He borrowed everything: a place to be born, a place to sleep (on many nights He slept on the Mount of Olives), a boat to cross the Sea of Galilee in and preach from, an animal to ride on during His triumphal entry into Jerusalem, a room for the Passover, and a tomb to be buried in. The only person who ever lived on this earth who had the right to everything on it wound up with nothing. Though King of kings and Lord of lords, the rightful heir to David's throne, and God in human flesh, He had no advantages or privileges in this world. He was given little, yet served everyone. That was the incredible destiny of the One of whom it is written, "All things came into being through Him; and apart from Him nothing came into being that has come into being" (John 1:3).

Christ's instruction and example of service for us is clear. After washing the disciples' feet, He said, "If I then, the Lord and the Teacher, washed your feet, you also ought to wash one another's feet. For I gave you an example that you also should do as I did to you" (13:14-15).

Christ Identified with Sinners

Christ's service to sinners took the form of total identification. Paul says that He "was made in the likeness of men" (Phil. 2:7). He was given all the essential attributes of humanity, thus He became like us. He was a genuine human, not just a facsimile. He was more than God in a body—He became the God-man, being fully God and fully man. And like a man, Jesus was born and increased in wisdom and physical maturity (see Luke 2:52).

When Jesus became a man, He took on the nature of man in his fallen and weakened condition: He hurt, He wept, He hungered, He thirsted, He tired, and He died. He was burdened with the results of man's Fall.[4]

When Christ took on human nature in its fallen character, it was with one significant element eliminated: sin. Jesus was "tempted in all things as we are, yet without sin" (Heb. 4:15). Although Christ never sinned, He felt the results of the Fall when He became one of us. Jesus "had to be made like His brethren in all things, so that He might become a merciful and faithful high priest" (2:17). For Christ to feel what we feel, He needed to be made like us. He experienced all the tests and temptations we do, but never gave in to sin. That's why He's such a faithful and understanding High Priest.

Christ Looked Like a Man

The next step in Christ's descent relates closely to the previous point. Christ was not only "made in the likeness of men" (Phil. 2:7), but also "found in appearance as a man" (v. 8). The difference between these two phrases is simply a shift in focus. In verse 8 we see the humiliation of Christ from the vantage point of those who saw and experienced Him. Christ was the God-man, but as people looked at Him they saw the appearance (Greek, *schema*, "outward form") of a man. Thus they viewed Him as no different than any other man.

For Christ to become man was humbling enough. For Him not to be recognized as the Messiah must have been even more humbling. He performed miracles and taught authoritatively, yet these were typical responses: "You are a Samaritan and have a demon" (John 8:48), and "Is not this Jesus, the son of Joseph, whose father and mother we know? How does He now say, 'I have come down out of heaven'?" (6:42). Because their minds were darkened by their sin, people recognized His humanity but could not see His deity. They treated the King of kings not only like a man, but also like the worst of men—a common criminal.

Christ Humbled Himself

Instead of fighting back, Christ "humbled Himself" (Phil. 2:8). Consider His trial. Despite unbelievable humiliation, He didn't speak a word in His defense except to agree with His accusers' statements: "You have said it yourself" (Matt. 26:64). They mocked Him, punched Him, pulled out His beard, treated Him as scum, yet He remained silent and accepted man's abuse through each phase of the trial. He did not demand His rights, but humbled Himself.

That kind of attitude is certainly lacking in our society. The demand for one's rights echoes throughout the corridors of our courts, the halls of our government, and even from the pews of our churches. What a different example Christ sets. As King, He could have demanded a palace, a chariot, servants, a fine wardrobe, and a kingdom full of jewels. But He lived as a simple man. Just think that the God of the universe stood beside Joseph and helped him in his carpenter shop in Nazareth!

Christ Was Obedient to the Point of Death

Christ's humility extended far beyond His poverty and simple way of life; He was willing to die for sinners: "Greater love has no one than this, that one lay down his life for his friends" (John 15:13). Christ volunteered to die—no man took His life from Him (see 10:18). He gave Himself up to an undeserved death.

Christ stooped to die for sinners because that was the way sinful men and women had to be saved. There was no other way to deliver them since "the wages of sin is death" (Rom. 6:23). God's holiness required that His wrath be satisfied, and that required a sacrifice. For Christ to help sinful man meant that He would have to die in the sinner's place and pay the penalty for sin so that He might lead us out of death and into eternal life.

Christ Died on a Cross

"Even death on a cross" (Phil. 2:8) calls attention to the most shocking feature of Christ's humiliation. He suffered not just death, but death on a cross—the most excruciating, embarrassing, degrading, painful and cruel death ever devised.

Crucifixion originated with the Persians and was later adopted by the Romans. They used this method to execute rebellious slaves and the worst of criminals. The Jews hated that form of punishment because Deuteronomy 21:23 said, "Anyone who is hung on a tree is under God's curse" (*NIV*). Galatians 3:13 says, "Christ redeemed us from the curse of the Law, having become a curse for us— for it is written, 'Cursed is every one who hangs on a tree.' " The God who created the universe suffered the ultimate human degradation—hanging naked before a mocking world, with nails driven through His hands and feet.

The grace and love of God toward sinners was such that Christ stooped to die for them. At the end of Paul's doctrinal survey of salvation in Romans, he said, "Oh, the depth of the riches both of the wisdom and knowledge of God! How unsearchable are His judgments and unfathomable His ways!" (11:33). He was in awe of God's plan of salvation—a plan no man would have dreamed to devise.

If we had planned the Incarnation, we probably would have designed for Christ to be born in a palace. Of necessity His family would have been wealthy and prominent, and He would have been educated in the finest universities and taught by the most erudite scholars. We would have orchestrated events so that everyone loved, revered, honored and respected Him. He would have traveled in all the prominent circles and conversed with the most influential people.

We certainly would not have had Him born in a stable to a poor family. He would not have wasted His youth in a carpenter's shop in some obscure town. No ragtag band would have sufficed as His followers—only the elite could have served Him as His disciples.

Ultimately, we would never have allowed Him to be humiliated. We would have imprisoned or executed anyone who spit on Him, mocked Him or hurt Him. Lest you think you wouldn't have planned it that way, just recall that Peter was prepared to stop the Lord from carrying out the plan of salvation. He rebuked Christ, saying, "God forbid it, Lord! This shall never happen to You" (Matt. 16:22). Yet any plan for the coming of the Messiah that differed from God's would have resulted in the salvation of not one soul. No wonder the psalmist said, "Your judgments are like a great deep" (Ps. 36:6). God's ways are unsearchable, His truths profound. And as deep as God's divine purpose is, it was accomplished in Christ on our behalf.

Benjamin Warfield, the great theologian, offers a fitting conclusion to remind us of what the Lord Jesus Christ did for us:

> We see Him among the thousands of Galilee, anointed of God with the Holy Ghost and power, going about doing good: with no pride of birth, though He was a king; with no pride of intellect, though omniscience dwelt within Him; with no pride of power, though all power in heaven and earth was in His hands; or of station, though the fullness of the Godhead dwelt in Him bodily; or of superior goodness or holiness: but in lowliness of mind esteeming every one better than Himself, healing the sick, casting out devils, feeding the hungry, and everywhere breaking to men the bread of life. We see Him everywhere offering to men His life for the salvation of their souls: and when, at last, the forces of evil gathered thick around Him, walking, alike without display and without dismay, the path of

suffering appointed for Him, and giving His life at Calvary that through His death the world might live.[5]

Since Christ, the God of the universe, willingly gave up so much for you, what ought you to give up for Him? The least any believer can do is give up what he holds most dear to love and serve the One who can't be anything but most dear and precious to him. Return to the joy of your first love and experience once again the internal joy that comes from knowing you are rightly related to the Lord and Savior.

Notes

1. C. S. Lewis, *The Grand Miracle* (New York: Macmillan, 1960), pp. 111-112.
2. See William Barclay, *The Letters to the Philippians, Colossians, and Thessalonians* (Philadelphia, PA: Westminster, 1976), p. 35.
3. James Hope Moulton and George Milligan, *The Vocabulary of the Greek Testament* (Grand Rapids, MI: Eerdmans, 1930), p. 417.
4. See William Hendricksen, *New Testament Commentary: Exposition of Philippians* (Grand Rapids, MI: Baker Books, 1962), p. 110.
5. Benjamin Warfield, *The Person and Work of Christ* (Philadelphia, PA: Presbyterian and Reformed Press, 1950), pp. 563-564.

THE SUFFERING
SERVANT

In his devotional studies on the life of Christ, titled *The Second Person,* commentator Lehman Strauss writes:

> Not one person in all the world is exempt from sorrow.
> Philosophers of every age have acknowledged it. Biographers, no matter how shallow the treatise, have recorded it.
> Experience has confirmed it. From the fact of suffering there
> is no escape. It sinks its fangs deeply into rich and poor,
> high and low, saved and lost.
>
> Except for natural causes and war, perhaps the greatest
> injuries have been inflicted upon men because of their religious convictions. Since the vicious slaying of John the
> Baptist . . . there has been no intermission in the attacks on
> the followers of Christ. History is revealing in its gruesome
> accounts of human suffering inflicted upon thousands of
> His disciples.[1]

While that is what we most often associate with those who suffer for Christ, Strauss identifies a subtler, but nonetheless real, type
of suffering:

> There is the torture of the mind and the agony of the soul—
> that escapeless, gnawing suffering which no person can
> truly share. Records of this are uncommon; words do not

adequately portray it. Are you brokenhearted because one with whom you shared your confidences has betrayed you?

Are you misunderstood and do your associates not value your taste nor your choices? . . . Have friends or loved ones forsaken you? . . . Do others torment you until you sting with shame? . . . Do the injustices done you inflame you until you think you must retaliate? . . . Do you believe no one cares? . . . Do you feel that the burden you must carry is too great?[2]

In our safe, secure society, it is unlikely we will ever suffer to the same degree as the martyrs and saints did who came before us, yet to those last series of questions Strauss posed, we all can relate. Every Christian has experienced at least one if not all those types of sorrows throughout his or her lifetime. How we respond is the true test of our faith and will reveal the depth of our relationship to Christ.

The Reality of Suffering

The Christian life is a call to glory through a journey of suffering. That's because those in Christ are inevitably at odds with their culture and society, since all Satan-energized systems actively oppose Christ and His followers. The apostle John said a person can't love both God and the world (see 1 John 2:15), and James said that "whoever wishes to be a friend of the world makes himself an enemy of God" (Jas. 4:4).

Those who love Christ are an open rebuke to the society in which they live. That was the apostle Peter's point when he described Christians as "a chosen race, a royal priesthood, a holy nation, a people for God's own possession . . . [who] proclaim the excellencies of Him who [called them] out of darkness into His marvelous light" (1 Pet. 2:9). Our dark world will resent and be hostile toward anyone who represents the Lord Jesus Christ in that way. That resentment and hostility may be felt at certain times and places more than others, but it is always present to some extent.

Fortunately, we have One to whom we can turn when we suffer—the very One who suffered for us: the Lord Jesus Christ. Peter documents for us the suffering of Jesus:

> For you have been called for this purpose, since Christ also suffered for you, leaving you an example for you to follow in His steps, who committed no sin, nor was any deceit found in His mouth; and while being reviled, He did not revile in return; while suffering, He uttered no threats, but kept entrusting Himself to Him who judges righteously (1 Pet. 2:21-23).

Peter's model of how to respond to suffering was Jesus Christ, and we need to follow His example. Verse 21 begins with the phrase "For you have been called for this purpose." The connective "for" points back to the last part of verse 20: "If when you do what is right and suffer for it you patiently endure it, this finds favor with God." Christians are to endure suffering because it pleases God. Verse 21 amplifies that idea by stating that Christians are specifically called to suffer.

A Christian's call to glory necessitates walking the path of suffering. First Peter 5:10 explains why: "After you have suffered for a little while, the God of all grace, who called you to His eternal glory in Christ, will Himself perfect, confirm, strengthen and establish you." Suffering is God's way of maturing His people spiritually. He is pleased when we patiently endure the suffering that comes our way.

Peter also said, "You greatly rejoice, even though now for a little while, if necessary, you have been distressed by various trials, so that the proof of your faith, being more precious than gold which is perishable, even though tested by fire, may be found to result in praise and glory and honor at the revelation of Jesus Christ" (1:6-7). God allows suffering as a validation of our faith and to increase our capacity to praise, glorify and honor God.

Many believers take the wrong approach and look for explanations for their trials elsewhere. Yet it is through those very trials that we deepen our bond with Christ. In Him only can we find the inner peace and joy to see our trials through to the end (see Jas. 1:2-3). Rejoicing in our first love helps us view our trials from our Lord's perspective.

That was what Paul was aiming at when he said that our "momentary, light affliction is producing for us an eternal weight of glory far beyond all comparison" (2 Cor. 4:17). Suffering does make us stronger so that it affects how we will function later. That's why Paul went on to say our focus isn't on the present but on the future: "We look not at the things which are seen, but at the things which are not seen; for the things which are seen are temporal, but the things which are not seen are eternal" (v. 18). In other words, as you endure a trial, focus on its eternal impact, not its temporary consequence.

Christ Himself understood that this was God's plan. To the disciples on the road to Emmaus, He said, "O foolish men and slow of heart to believe in all that the prophets have spoken! Was it not necessary for the Christ to suffer these things and to enter into His glory?" (Luke 24:25-26). If our Lord had to suffer to enter into His future glory, we ought to expect to suffer as well. That is why Peter said, "You have been called for this purpose, since Christ also suffered for you, leaving you an example for you to follow in His steps" (1 Pet. 2:21).

The Pattern of Suffering

The path to glory for Christ was the path of unjust suffering, and that's to be our path as well. Because our Lord endured suffering with perfect patience and was exalted to the highest point of glory, He is our example of how to respond to suffering. He sets the standard for us.

Jesus was executed as a criminal on a cross. Yet He was guilty of no crime—no wrong, no trespass, no sin. He never had an evil thought or spoke an evil word. His was the most unjust execution ever perpetrated on a human being. Yet from it we learn that even though a person may be perfectly within the will of God—greatly loved and gifted, perfectly righteous and obedient—he may still experience unjust suffering. Like Jesus, he may be misunderstood, misrepresented, hated, persecuted, and even murdered. In His death Christ set the standard of how to respond to unjust persecution.

Following His Pattern

The Greek word translated "example" (*hupogrammos*) in 1 Peter 2:21 refers to a pattern that is placed under a piece of paper as the object to be traced. Like children who learn their letters by tracing them over a pattern, we are to trace our lives according to the pattern Jesus Christ has laid down for us.

We follow His pattern by walking "in His steps." "Steps" translates the Greek word *ichnos*, which refers to a track or line of footprints. We are to walk in Christ's footprints because He traveled a righteous path, and along that path He endured unjust suffering. Some suffer more than others, but all who follow Christ will experience suffering to some degree.

The writer of Hebrews emphasized this particular role of Christ when he said, "It was fitting for [God] . . . in bringing many sons to glory, to perfect the author of their salvation through sufferings" (2:10). The Greek word for "author" is *archegos*, which literally means "pioneer" or "leader." This word was commonly used in classical Greek of a pioneer who blazed a trail for others to follow. The *archegos* never stood at the rear giving orders; he was always out front leading and setting the example. Christ is our supreme pioneer, our perfect leader and example, who leads us down the path of suffering and to victory on the other side.

Following His Reactions

Our Lord's suffering on the cross was certainly prominent in Peter's mind because he personally witnessed his Lord's pain, though from afar. In 1 Peter 2:22-23, he takes us to the cross, explaining in the process the meaning of Isaiah 53—the clearest Old Testament chapter on the suffering of the Messiah.

He Committed No Sin in Word or Deed

Peter first says that Christ "committed no sin, nor was any deceit found in His mouth" (1 Pet. 2:22). Isaiah 53:9 says that "He [the Messiah] had done no violence." "Violence" is translated "lawlessness" in the Septuagint, the Greek version of the Hebrew Old Testament. The translators understood that the violence spoken of in Isaiah 53:9 is violence, or sin, against God's law, which "is lawlessness" (1 John 3:4). Peter, under the inspiration of the Holy Spirit, understood the violence spoken of in Isaiah 53:9 in the same way. Peter's point is that in spite of the unjust treatment Christ had to endure, He committed no sin. He was impeccable—He did not and could not sin (see 1 Pet. 1:19).

Isaiah 53:9 adds, "Nor was there any deceit in His mouth." That strengthens the idea that Jesus committed no sin because sin easily manifests itself in what we say. The Hebrew word translated "deceit" can refer to any sin of the tongue, such as deception, innuendo or slander.

What we say, more than any other aspect of human behavior, reveals what's in our hearts (see Mark 7:21). That's what led James to say, "If anyone does not stumble in what he says, he is a perfect man" (Jas. 3:2). Jesus never offended in what He said, indicating He is a perfect man.

In all the circumstances of His ministry on earth, our Lord was absolutely sinless: He was "tempted in all things as we are, yet without sin" (Heb. 4:15; see also 2 Cor. 5:21; Heb. 7:26). Consequently He was the most unjustly treated person who ever lived. He is the perfect model of how we are to respond to unjust treatment because He endured far worse treatment than any person who will ever live, yet He never sinned.

He Didn't Strike Back

Peter next reflected on what Isaiah 53:7 says of the Messiah: "He was oppressed and He was afflicted, yet He did not open His mouth; like a lamb that is led to slaughter, and like a sheep that is silent before its shearers, so He did not open His mouth." That reflects the attitude of Jesus before His tormentors: "While being reviled, He did not revile in return" (1 Pet. 2:23). Though under sustained provocation, Jesus spoke no evil.

The Greek word translated "reviled" pictures the continual piling up of one abuse on top of another. Jesus was consistent in His response to such treatment: He was silent (see Matt. 26:57-68; 27:11-14; Mark 14:53-65; 15:1-5; Luke 23:8-9). Christians, like their Master, are never to abuse those who abuse them.

He Didn't Make Threats

Jesus "uttered no threats" in the face of incredible suffering (1 Pet. 2:23). He was spit on, His beard was pulled out, a crown of thorns was crushed onto His head, and nails were driven through His flesh to pin Him to a cross. In any other innocent person such unjust treatment would have fostered some kind of retaliation, but not in Christ. He was the Incarnate God—the Creator and Sustainer of the universe—and as such had the power to send His tormentors into eternal flames. Yet instead of threatening them, He said, "Father, forgive them; for they do not know what they are doing" (Luke 23:34). Christ died for sinners, including those who persecuted Him. He knew that the glory of salvation could be achieved only through the path of suffering, so He accepted His suffering without bitterness, anger, or a spirit of retaliation.

He Entrusted Himself to God

First Peter 3:9 says that Christians are not to be "returning evil for evil or insult for insult, but giving a blessing instead." That was Jesus' attitude: He "kept entrusting Himself to Him who judges righteously" (2:23). The word translated "entrusting" (Greek *paradidomi*) means "to hand over for someone to keep." In every instance of suffering, our Lord handed over the circumstance and Himself to God.

Christ's last words on the cross reveal His trust in God: "Father, into Your hands I commit My spirit" (Luke 23:46). He was confident in God's righteous judgment and the glory that would be His. That allowed Him to calmly accept tremendous suffering. We are to respond in the same way when confronted with unjust persecution on the job or in our families or other relationships. When we retaliate we forfeit the blessing and reward that suffering is meant to bring. A retaliatory spirit exposes our lack of confidence in God's ability to make things right in His own time, which will include punishing the unjust and rewarding those who are faithful in suffering. That kind of response also calls into question the reality of our commitment to Christ. Unbelievers will be turned off by those who claim to love Christ yet act like any other unregenerate person. All Christians need to remember that leaving your first love may have eternal ramifications. Bible commentator Alan Stibbs wrote:

> In . . . the unique instance of our Lord's passion, when the sinless One suffered as if He were the worst of sinners, and bore the extreme penalty of sin, there is a double sense in which He may have acknowledged God as the righteous Judge. On the one hand, because voluntarily, and in fulfillment of God's will, He was taking the sinner's place and bearing sin, He did not protest at what He had to suffer. Rather He consciously recognized that it was the penalty righteously due to sin. So He handed Himself over to be punished. He recognized that in letting such shame, pain and curse fall upon Him, the righteous God was judging righteously. On the other hand, because He Himself was sinless, He also believed that in due time God, as the righteous Judge, would vindicate Him as righteous, and exalt Him from the grave, and reward Him for what He had willingly endured for others' sake by giving Him the right completely to save them from the penalty and power of their own wrongdoing.[3]

When we entrust ourselves to God as the righteous judge, we are following Christ's example by looking to God for vindication, exaltation and reward.

If you're a Christian, expect to suffer. As believers, we are aliens and strangers in the world, waging war against fleshly lusts and being slandered and persecuted. We must expect to suffer in the name of the One who endured all manner of suffering for us. The central thrust of Peter's message is to remind us of the necessity of suffering. When in the midst of suffering we sin in thought, word or deed by retaliating, we lose our victory and damage our testimony.

I believe that in days to come Christians will become increasingly unpopular with secular society. Strong stands for the truth of Scripture and the gospel message may soon become intolerable. That will result in unjust treatment.

The prospect of such treatment ought to drive us to passages like 1 Peter 2:21-23 for reassurance. Here we learn that, like our Lord, we are to walk the path of suffering to attain the glory of reward and exaltation in the future. That realization surely prompted the martyr Stephen to fix his eyes on Jesus in glory and ask God to forgive his murderers (see Acts 7:54-60). Stephen entrusted himself to God, knowing that the Lord would vindicate him.

In May 1555, Bishop Hugh Latimer, soon to be burned at the stake for his antipapal, Reformed convictions, wrote, "Die once we must; how and where, we know not. . . . Here is not our home; let us therefore accordingly consider things, having always before our eyes that heavenly Jerusalem, and the way thereto in persecution."[4] Later that year both Latimer and his friend Ridley were fed to the flames, but not until Latimer—astonishingly composed—said to his colleague, "Be of good comfort, Master Ridley, and play the man. We shall this day light such a candle, by God's grace, in England, as I trust shall never be put out."[5]

If we are ever to deepen our relationship to Christ, we must be willing to share in His sufferings. That was certainly Paul's perspective when he said, "That I may know Him and the power of His resurrection and the fellowship of His sufferings, being conformed to His death" (Phil. 3:10). Any vital, dynamic relationship is necessarily characterized by a willingness to share in all life's experiences, whether good or bad.

You may never have the opportunity to glorify God in the manner Latimer did, yet as you remember how Christ suffered for you, I hope you'll regard each momentary light affliction God brings your way as an opportunity to glorify Christ. You don't have to seek abuse, but be faithful to exalt Christ no matter where you are. When the suffering comes, God will be gracious. And when you endure it with patience, you will reap maturity in Christ for the present and a greater capacity to glorify God in the life to come. Charles Haddon Spurgeon understood that when he said:

> When the pangs shoot through our body, and ghastly death appears in view, people see the patience of the dying Christian. *Our infirmities become the black velvet on which the diamond of God's love glitters all the more brightly.* Thank God I can suffer! Thank God I can be made the object of shame and contempt, for in this way God shall be glorified.[6]

Notes

1. Lehman Strauss, *The Second Person* (New York: Loizeaux Brothers, 1951), pp. 113-114.
2. Ibid., p. 114.
3. Alan Stibbs, *The First Epistle General of Peter* (Grand Rapids, MI: Eerdmans, 1971), p. 119.
4. Bishop Hugh Latimer, cited in Harold S. Darby, *Hugh Latimer* (London: Epworth, 1953), p. 237.
5. Ibid., p. 247.
6. Charles Haddon Spurgeon, cited in Tom Carter, *Spurgeon at His Best* (Grand Rapids, MI: Baker Books, 1988), p. 202, emphasis added.

OUR LOVING SUBSTITUTE

Tribes once roamed the Russian expanse much like Indian tribes roamed the Americas. The tribes that controlled the best hunting grounds and the choicest natural resources were often led by the strongest and wisest leaders. I was told the story of one particular tribe whose success was due largely to the fairness and wisdom of the laws established and enforced by its great leader.

One day it was reported that someone in the tribe was stealing. The leader issued a proclamation that the thief, when captured, would receive 10 lashes from the tribal whip master. Despite the warning, the thievery continued, even as the leader upped the level of punishment. Eventually he stopped raising that level once it reached 40 lashes, knowing that only he could survive such a severe lashing. One day the thief was finally apprehended, and to the horror of everyone, the thief turned out to be the leader's own aged mother.

The people speculated what the leader would do. One of his laws required children to love and honor their parents, yet another demanded the public whipping of thieves. Great arguments arose as the day of judgment approached. Would he satisfy his love and save his mother, or would he satisfy his law and watch his mother die under the whip?

Finally the day came. The tribe gathered around the great compound, in the center of which stood a large post. The leader soon entered and sat down on his throne. Then two towering warriors led his frail mother into the compound and tied her to the post. Finally the tribal whip master, a powerful man with bulging muscles, entered carrying a long leather whip. As he approached the little woman, the warriors ripped off her garment, exposing her frail back.

The whip master took his stance. His great arm cracked the whip in the air as he prepared to bring the first lash upon her. Just then the leader held up his hand to halt the punishment. A sigh of relief went up from the table. His love would be satisfied, but what about his law?

The leader rose from his throne and strode toward his mother. As he walked he removed his own shirt, tossing it aside. He then wrapped his great arms around his mother, exposing his huge muscular back to the whip master. Breaking the heavy silence he commanded, "Proceed with the punishment."

That wonderful story illustrates what Christ did for us. Like the leader's mother, our sin put us under the whip of judgment. Ezekiel warned that "the soul who sins will die" (Ezek. 18:4). The apostle Paul put it this way: "The wages of sin is death" (Rom. 6:23). Sin brings death, inevitably and without exception.

All men will die, and their death is set by divine appointment—an appointment everyone will keep. After death comes eternal judgment (see Heb. 9:27), and that too is appointed by God. Since men are unable to atone for their own sins, God's judgment demands that they pay or have a substitute pay for them.

Left to his own resources, therefore, man has no prospect but death. But God is also loving, and He had a plan to save man from hell—He supplied the Substitute who would satisfy His justice by taking the punishment of man on Himself and dying in his place. That was His design in sending Christ.

Like the leader in the story, Christ humbled Himself from His exalted throne and came to earth so that He could pay the penalty we owed just as the leader paid the penalty his mother owed. Jesus wrapped His arms around us, satisfying His love by enabling us to escape God's wrath, and satisfying His law by paying the penalty for our sin.

The substitutionary death of Christ is the essential truth of the Christian faith. Without it there is no gospel, no good news. Apart from His dying, we cannot escape the clutches of death and hell. British preacher Charles Haddon Spurgeon wrote:

> In one word, the great fact on which the Christian's hope rests is substitution. Christ's being made sin for us that we might be made the righteousness of God in him, Christ offering up a true and proper substitutionary sacrifice in the place of as many as the Father gave him, who are recognized by their trusting in him—this is the cardinal fact of the gospel.[1]

Commentator Leon Morris looked at this same truth from another perspective:

> To put it bluntly and plainly, if Christ is not my Substitute, I still occupy the place of a condemned sinner. If my sins and my guilt are not transferred to Him, if He did not take them upon Himself, then surely they remain with me. If He did not deal with my sins, I must face their consequences. If my penalty was not borne by Him, it still hangs over me.[2]

Scripture is filled with reminders of what believers were like prior to their salvation in Christ. Any attempt to reinvigorate our devotion to Christ must begin with a reminder of what He saved us from and the price He had to pay to rescue us. In this chapter we'll review what we were saved from, examine the ramifications of His substitutionary death for us, and our resulting righteousness.

Our Problem

The apostle Paul states so simply and profoundly our condition without Christ: "You were dead in your trespasses and sins" (Eph. 2:1; see also Col. 2:13). As we have seen, the wages, or payment, for sin is death (see Rom. 6:23), and because man is born in sin, death is his ultimate future. That's not to say he becomes spiritually dead because he sins; he is spiritually dead because by nature he is sinful. Except for Jesus Christ, that is the condition of every human being since the Fall.

Man's basic problem is not lack of harmony with his heritage or environment, as society would have you believe, but his total lack of harmony with his Creator, from whom he is alienated by sin (see Eph. 4:18). He is spiritually dead to all God offers, including righteousness, inner peace, and happiness, and ultimately every good thing. Apart from God, men are spiritual zombies—they are the walking dead who can't even know they are dead. They may go through the motions of life, but they certainly don't possess it.

Before we were saved, we were like every other person who is separate from God—"dead in . . . trespasses and sins" (Eph. 2:1). The Greek construction here is a locative of sphere, indicating the sphere, or realm, in which something or someone exists. We were dead not because we had committed sin but because we were *in* sin. Committing sinful acts does not make us sinners; we commit sinful acts because we *are* sinners.

By stating that we were all dead in "trespasses *and* sins," Paul was not describing two different kinds of wrongdoing but simply referring to the breadth of our sinfulness. "Trespasses" refers to stumbling, falling, or going in the wrong direction. The Greek word translated "sins" (*hamartia*) originally meant "to miss the mark," as when a hunter with bow and arrow missed his target. Eventually it was applied to missing or falling short of any goal or standard. In the spiritual realm it refers to falling short of God's standard of holiness: "All have sinned and fall short of the glory of God" (Rom. 3:23). Sin is falling short of God's glory, and falling short of God's glory is sin.

Jesus reiterated God's standard when He commanded that we be perfect, just as our Father in heaven is perfect (see Matt. 5:48). God's command to "be holy; for I am holy" (Lev. 11:44; see also 1 Pet. 1:16) did not create a new standard for mankind; He has never had any other standard for man but perfect holiness.

God's perfect standard of holiness is ever before man. No matter how much good he does or attempts to do, the standard of never doing or never having done evil at all is unattainable.

The fact is that while we may be Christians now, we used to walk "according to the course of this world, according to the prince of the power of the air, of the spirit that is now working in the sons of disobedience. Among them we too all formerly lived in the lusts of our flesh, indulging the desires of the flesh and of the mind, and were by nature children of wrath, even as the rest" (Eph. 2:1-3). We used to think and live according to the world's standards, which are dominated and controlled by Satan. Following his lead, sinful men and women adopt the goals and values of a system intent on defying God and elevating self.

As a result, they live "in the lusts of [their] flesh, indulging the desires of the flesh and of the mind" (v. 3). "Lusts" refers to strong desires of every sort, not just sexual lust, while "desires" emphasizes strong willfulness, a seeking after something with great diligence. Those terms are used synonymously to represent fallen man's complete orientation to his own selfish way. By nature he is driven to fulfill the lusts and desires of his sinful flesh and mind, completely selfish and abandoned to doing whatever feels good and resolutely defying God.

In writing to the Colossian believers, Paul describes their condition as "formerly alienated and hostile in mind, engaged in evil deeds" (Col. 1:21). The Greek word translated "alienated" (*apallotioo*) means "estranged" or "separated." Before their reconciliation, the Colossians were completely estranged from God because of their sin. They were also "hostile in mind" or "hateful." Unbelievers also hate God; they resent His holy standards and commands because they are "engaged in evil deeds." Scripture teaches that unbelievers love "the darkness rather than the Light, for their deeds [are] evil. For everyone who does evil hates the Light, and does not come to the Light for fear that his deeds will be exposed" (John 3:19-20). Their problem is not ignorance, but willful love of sin.

Sin is the root cause of man's alienation from God. Since God cannot fellowship with sin (see Hab. 1:13; 1 John 1:6), sin must be dealt with before God and man can be reconciled. From God's holy perspective, His just wrath against sin must be appeased.

Apart from gracious reconciliation through Christ, every person by nature is the object of God's wrath—a victim of His eternal condemnation and judgment. Since that is a Christian's former condition, why would any believer leave the loving relationship he has with Christ to pursue again the very thing Christ saved him from? Yet that is what many Christians do today. As you look again at what Christ accomplished on your behalf, I hope you'll be challenged to renew your commitment to love Him above all else.

Our Substitute

Before you became a Christian, you stood with every other unbeliever under God's condemning hand—an enemy with seemingly no possibility of escape from His judgment. Your sin declared you guilty before God, and there was no price you could pay that could cancel your debt to Him. No hope would have been the best way to describe your dilemma, and that's just what Scripture says, "Remember that you were . . . separate from Christ . . . having no hope and without God in the world" (Eph. 2:12).

When you and I were at our most desperate, when nothing we could do could save us, God did: "But God, being rich in mercy, because of His great love with which He loved us, even when we were dead in our transgressions, made us alive together with Christ" (Eph. 2:4-5). Simply because God loved us, He provided a way for us to return to Him. Even though we sinned against Him, through His rich mercy and great love He offered forgiveness and reconciliation to us, just as He does to every repentant sinner.

God loved enough not only to forgive but also to die for the very ones who had offended Him. Paul writes, "For while we were still helpless, at the right time Christ died for the ungodly" (Rom. 5:6). Since we were helpless to bring ourselves to God, He sent His only begotten Son, Jesus Christ, to die for us, notwithstanding the fact that we were ungodly and completely unworthy of His love. When we were powerless to escape from sin and death, helpless against Satan's schemes, and unable to please God in any way, He still sent His Son to die on our behalf. In that one act He proved the wonders of His love: "Greater love has no one than this, that one lay down his life for his friends" (John 15:13). Compassionate love for those who don't deserve it made salvation possible.

Regarding this great love, Paul writes, "God demonstrates His own love toward us, in that while we were yet sinners, Christ died for us" (Rom. 5:8). That sort of selfless, undeserved love is completely beyond our limited, finite comprehension. Yet that is the very love the just and infinitely holy God had toward us even while we were still sinners. When we were still hopelessly enmeshed in our sin, God sent His Son to die in our place.

The apostle Peter says, "He Himself bore our sins in His body on the cross, so that we might die to sin and live to righteousness; for by His wounds you were healed" (1 Pet. 2:24). That description of Christ's death on our behalf is an allusion to Isaiah's description of the substitutionary, sin-bearing death of the Messiah (see Isa. 53:4-5,11). To emphasize this substitutionary nature of Christ's death, Peter says that He "died for sins once for all, the just for the unjust" (1 Pet. 3:18).

The apostle Paul also emphasized the substitutionary work of Christ. He said that God "made Him who knew no sin to be sin on our behalf, that we might become the righteousness of God in Him" (2 Cor. 5:21) and that "Christ redeemed us from the curse of the Law, having become a curse for us" (Gal. 3:13).

Some claim it's immoral to teach that God would take on human flesh and bear the sins of men and women in their stead. They say it defies justice to transfer the penalty of sin from a guilty person to an innocent person. But that's not what happened on the cross. Commentator Leon Morris explains what God did:

> In the process of salvation God is not transferring penalty from one man (guilty) to another man (innocent). He is bearing it Himself. The absolute oneness between the Father and the Son in the work of the atonement must not for a moment be lost sight of. When Christ substitutes for

sinful man in His death that is God Himself bearing the consequences of our sin, God saving man at cost to Himself, not at cost to someone else. As Leonard Hodgson puts it, "He wills that sin shall be punished, but He does not will that sin shall be punished without also willing that the punishment shall fall on Himself." In part the atonement is to be understood as a process whereby God absorbs in Himself the consequences of man's sin.[3]

On the cross Christ willingly took our sin and bore its penalty. Nothing was forced on Him. If He had not willed to take our sin and accept its punishment, as sinners we would have borne the punishment of sin in hell forever. Christ's work on the cross wasn't unfair—it was God's love in action!

First Peter 2:24 says that Christ "Himself bore our sins." "Himself" is emphatic in the text—it was Christ *Himself* who took on sin and bore its penalty. He bore it willingly and voluntarily, and He bore it alone. He indeed was "the Lamb of God who takes away the sin of the world!" (John 1:29).

When Peter said He "bore" our sins, he used a term that means "to carry a massive, heavy weight." That's what sin is. It's so heavy that Romans 8:22 says, "The whole creation groans and suffers" under its weight. Only Jesus could remove such a weight from us, and He did so by bearing our sins "in His body on the cross." It was God's plan that Christ be lifted up to die (see John 12:32-33). Paul says that Christ had to be hung on a tree to fulfill the prediction of becoming a curse for us (see Deut. 21:23; Gal. 3:13). So Jesus bore our sins by enduring the wrath of God as He was suspended on a cross of wood.

To better understand just what Christ accomplished for us on that cross, we need to examine the different terms that express the ramifications of Christ's substitutionary death. Several key words describe the richness of our salvation in Christ: *redemption* and its corollary *forgiveness, justification* and *reconciliation*. In redemption, the sinner stands before God as a slave, but is granted his freedom (see Rom. 6:18-22). In forgiveness, the sinner stands before God as a debtor, but the debt is paid and forgotten (see Eph. 1:7). In justification the sinner, though standing before God guilty and condemned, is declared righteous (see Rom. 8:33). In reconciliation, the sinner stands before God as an enemy, but becomes His friend (see 2 Cor. 5:18-20). Leon Morris highlights the importance of those terms in this manner:

> Redemption is substitutionary, for it means that Christ paid the price that we could not pay, paid it in our stead, and we go free. Justification interprets our salvation judicially, and as the New Testament sees it Christ took our legal liability, took it in our stead. Reconciliation means the making of people to be at one by the taking away of the cause of hostility. In this case the cause is sin, and Christ removed that cause for us. We could not deal with sin. He could and did, and did it in such a way that it is reckoned to us. Was there a price to be paid? He paid it. Was there a victory to be won? He won it. Was there a penalty to be borne? He bore it. Was there a judgment to be faced? He faced it.[4]

Redemption

Scripture speaks eloquently of our redemption from sin. In Romans Paul describes redemption as our "having been freed from sin" and becoming "slaves of righteousness" (6:18). In Galatians he says that Jesus Christ "gave Himself for our sins, so that He might rescue us from this present evil age, according to the will of our God and Father" (1:4). In Colossians he says that God "rescued us from the domain of darkness, and transferred us to the kingdom of His beloved Son, in whom we have redemption, the forgiveness of sins" (1:13-14). And in Ephesians he writes, "In Him [Christ] we have redemption through His blood, the forgiveness of our trespasses" (1:7).

Two Greek legal terms define redemption: *Agorazo* and the related *exagorazo* referred to buying or purchasing. In the New Testament they are used to denote spiritual purchase or redemption (see Gal. 3:13; Rev. 5:9). The other term for redemption, *lutroo* (along with its related forms), meant "to release from captivity."

An intensified form, *apolutrosis* (translated "redemption" in Eph. 1:7), was used to refer to paying a ransom to release someone from bondage, especially those under the yoke of slavery.

During New Testament times the Roman Empire had as many as six million slaves, and the buying and selling of them was big business. If someone wanted to free a loved one or friend who was a slave, he would buy him and then grant him his freedom. He would attest to that deliverance with a written certificate. *Lutroo* was used to designate such a transaction.

That is precisely the idea expressed in the New Testament use of the term to represent Christ's atoning sacrifice on the cross. Picture sin as man's captor and slave owner, demanding a price for his release, with death as the price. Biblical redemption is the act by which God Himself pays the ransom price to satisfy His own holy justice and to buy back fallen men and women and set them free from their sin.

The Redeemer

Jesus Christ is our Redeemer from sin—He paid the price for our release from iniquity and death. Because we now belong to Christ, by faith made one with Him, we are now acceptable to God. Every Christian is God's beloved child because the Lord Jesus Christ has become our Redeemer. The Hebrew concept of a kinsman-redeemer (see Ruth) set forth three qualifications: (1) The redeemer had to be related to the one needing redemption, (2) be able to pay the price, and (3) be willing to do so. The Lord Jesus Christ perfectly met those requirements.

The Redeemed

Those receiving redemption are the "we" of Ephesians 1:7—"the saints . . . who are faithful in Christ Jesus" (v. 1). Based on our earlier discussion in this chapter, we are acutely aware of our need for redemption. We were once sinners and desperate for a Redeemer. We can thank God that Christ "gave Himself for us, that He might redeem us from every lawless deed and purify for Himself a people for His own possession, zealous for good deeds" (Titus 2:14).

The Redemption Price

The price of our redemption is "His blood" (Eph. 1:7). It cost the blood of the Son of God to buy men back from the slave market of sin. Shedding of blood is a term not limited to the fluid, but a metonym for Christ's violent death on the cross. Scripture shows us that Christ gave not only His blood (see Acts 20:28), but also His very life (see Matt. 20:28) and self (see Gal. 1:4). Though stated differently, they all refer to Christ's death on our behalf. Through the sacrifice of His Son, God showed us mercy without violating His justice. Through His bloody death, our Lord poured out His life as a sacrificial, substitutionary payment for sin. That which we deserved and could not save ourselves from the beloved Savior, though He did not deserve it, took upon Himself. He made payment for what otherwise would have condemned us to death and hell.

We "were not redeemed with perishable things like silver or gold . . . but with precious blood, as of a lamb unblemished and spotless, the blood of Christ" (1 Pet. 1:18-19). No human, earthly commodity like silver or gold suffices to redeem man. Many today try, but all material things are perishable, subject to decay and corruption. No one can purchase redemption from sin by the payment of any perishable commodity.

But "the precious blood" of Christ could. Peter here compares the preciousness of Christ's death to that of an unblemished, spotless lamb—the finest, purest lamb any shepherd could own and the ultimate sacrifice any shepherd could make. Christ was the ultimate sacrifice of God, sufficient to redeem us from our bondage to sin. Christ was "the Lamb of God who takes away the sin of the world!" (John 1:29). The precious blood of Christ—emblematic of His sacrificial, substitutionary death—frees us from the guilt, condemnation, power and penalty of sin, and ultimately one glorious day will remove us from the presence of sin.

The Result: Forgiveness

The marvelous result of redemption for the believer is complete forgiveness of all sin. Speaking to the disciples about the Lord's Supper, Christ said, "This is My blood of the covenant, which is poured out for many for forgiveness of sins" (Matt. 26:28). Redemption brings forgiveness, because "without shedding of blood there is no forgiveness" (Heb. 9:22).

The Greek word often translated "forgiveness" (*aphiemi*) means "to send away never to return." Used as a legal term, it meant to repay or cancel a debt or to grant a pardon. Through the shedding of His own blood, Jesus Christ actually took the sins of the world upon His own head, as it were, and carried them an infinite distance away from where they could never return. Such is the extent of our forgiveness in Christ.

To illustrate how permanent our forgiveness in Christ is, Paul wrote the Colossians saying that when God forgave us, He "canceled out the certificate of debt consisting of decrees against us, which was hostile to us; and He has taken it out of the way, having nailed it to the cross" (2:14). "Certificate of debt" translates *cheirographos,* which literally means "something written with the hand." It was used to refer to a certificate of indebtedness handwritten by the debtor in acknowledgment of his debt.

Paul describes that certificate as "consisting of decrees against us." All people owe God a debt because they have violated His law. The certificate was "hostile to us" in that it was enough to condemn us to judgment and hell. But God canceled it out and wiped it away, like you would erase chalk off a blackboard. In that day, documents were commonly written either on papyrus, a paperlike material made from the bulrush plant, or vellum, which was made from an animal's hide. The ink they used contained no acid, thus it didn't soak into the material and could easily be wiped off if the scribe wanted to reuse the material. In a similar way, God has wiped off our certificate of debt, "having nailed it to the cross." Not a trace of it remains to be held against us.

That's why it is so tragic when so many Christians get depressed about their faults and failures, thinking and acting as if God still holds their sins against them. They have forgotten that since God has placed their sins upon Himself, they are separated from those sins "as far as the east is from the west" (Ps. 103:12). Before He even made the earth, He placed the sins of His elect on

His Son, who took them an eternal distance away. He dismissed our sins before we were born, and they can never return. "Therefore there is now no condemnation for those who are in Christ Jesus. For the law of the Spirit of life in Christ Jesus has set you free from the law of sin and of death" (Rom. 8:1-2). I hope you'll take to heart the fact that while forgiveness in Jesus Christ is undeserved, it is free and complete.

Finally, God's forgiveness is "according to the riches of His grace which He lavished upon us" (Eph. 1:7-8). God's grace is boundless, far beyond our ability to comprehend or describe, yet we know it is according to the boundless riches of that infinite grace that He provides forgiveness.

Justification

From redemption and forgiveness we move to the term that describes the judicial verdict of God on behalf of the redeemed sinner. The Greek word *dikaioo* and its related terms referred to legal acquittal of a charge and are used theologically to speak of a sinner's being vindicated, justified, and declared righteous before God.

Justification is God's declaration that all the demands of the law are fulfilled on behalf of the believing sinner through the righteousness of Jesus Christ. As a wholly forensic or legal transaction, justification changes the judicial *standing* of the sinner before God. In justification, God *imputes* the perfect righteousness of Christ to the believer's account, then declares the redeemed one fully righteous. Christ's own infinite merit is the ground on which the believer stands before God. Paul says that we have been "justified by His blood" (Rom. 5:9). Thus justification raises us to a level of complete acceptance and divine privilege in Christ. As a result, believers are not only perfectly free from any charge of guilt (see 8:33) but also have the full merit of Christ reckoned to their personal account (see 5:17). It is important to note, however, the distinction between justification and sanctification. In sanctification God actually *imparts* Christ's righteousness to the sinner. While the two must be distinguished, justification and sanctification can never be separated. God does not justify whom He does not sanctify.[5]

Reconciliation

The most immediate consequence of our justification is our reconciliation, which brings us peace with God. The Greek legal term translated "reconcile" (*katallasso*) meant to bring together two disputing parties. In the New Testament it is used to speak of a believer's reconciliation to God through Jesus Christ.

Because most unbelievers have no conscious hatred of God and don't actively oppose Him, they don't consider themselves to be His enemies. But the fact is that the mind of every unsaved person is self-centered and at peace only with the things of the flesh, and therefore by definition it is "hostile toward God" (Rom. 8:7). God is the enemy of the sinner, and that enmity cannot end unless and until the sinner places his trust in Jesus Christ.

Once a person embraces Christ in repentant faith, the sinless Son of God, who made perfect satisfaction for all our sins (an element of Christ's work that we'll examine in the next chapter), makes that person eternally at peace with God the Father. Beyond that "He Himself is our peace" (Eph. 2:14).

Full reconciliation with God is ours through the Lord Jesus. Because He possesses all the fullness of deity (see Col. 1:19), He is able to fully reconcile sinful men and women to God, "having made peace through the blood of His cross . . . [and] has now reconciled you in His fleshly body through death" (vv. 20,22). Only His violent death on the cross could effect our reconciliation with God. Those who trust in Christ are no longer God's enemies and no longer under His wrath, but are at peace with Him.

Perhaps no passage stresses the vital importance of reconciliation more than 2 Corinthians 5:17-21, in which we can discern five truths. First, reconciliation transforms men: "If any one is in Christ, he is a new creature; the old things passed away; behold, new things have come" (v. 17). Second, it appeases God's wrath: "He made Him who knew no sin to be sin on our behalf, so that we might become the righteousness of God in Him" (v. 21). Third, it comes through Christ: "All these things are from God, who reconciled us to Himself through Christ" (v. 18). Fourth, it is available to all who believe: "God was in Christ reconciling the world to

Himself" (v. 19). Finally, every believer has been given the ministry of proclaiming the message of reconciliation: God "gave us the ministry of reconciliation" (v. 18), and "He has committed to us the word of reconciliation" (v. 19).

God sends His people forth as ambassadors into a fallen, lost world, bearing amazing good news. People everywhere are hopelessly lost and doomed, cut off from God by sin. But God has provided the means of reconciliation through the death of His Son. Our mission is to plead with people to receive that reconciliation, before it is too late. Paul's attitude, expressed in verse 20, should be true of every believer: "Therefore, we are ambassadors for Christ, as though God were making an appeal through us; we beg you on behalf of Christ, be reconciled to God."

Our Righteousness

To be ambassadors, we must be able to live the part. And that was God's ultimate goal in effecting our redemption, justification and reconciliation. We just looked at 2 Corinthians 5:21, where Paul says, "He made Him who knew no sin to be sin on our behalf, that we might become the righteousness of God in Him." In Colossians 1:22 Paul says the goal of reconciliation is "to present you before Him holy and blameless and beyond reproach." And Peter says, "He Himself bore our sins in His body on the cross, so that we might die to sin and live to righteousness" (1 Pet. 2:24). Those verses don't claim that Christ died so that we could go to heaven, have peace, or experience love; He died to bring about a transformation: to make saints out of sinners.

The Greek word translated "die" (*apoginomai*) in 1 Peter 2:24 is used only here in the New Testament. It means "depart" or "cease existing." Christ's substitutionary work enables a person to depart from a life of sin and enter into an eternally new life pattern: a life of righteousness.

The apostle Paul said, "Our old self was crucified with [Christ], in order that our body of sin might be done away with, so that we should no longer be slaves to sin" (Rom. 6:6). Our identification with Christ in His death results in our walking "in newness of life" (v. 4). We have died to sin, thus it no longer has a claim on us. First Peter 2:24 echoes that thought: our identification with Christ in His death is a departure from sin and a new direction in life.

We began life as enemies of God, guilty of violating His standard of holiness, living a life of slavery to sin, and owing God a debt we could never repay. But through Christ, God bathed us in His love, offering up His Son as the ransom price in payment of our sin and thus accomplishing our redemption, forgiveness, justification and reconciliation.

If God so loved us, how can we not love Him and His Son with the depth of our whole being? What Christ accomplished for us deserves our utmost devotion. Anything less than undying love to Him depreciates His wondrous work on the cross. It is my sincere prayer that by continually remembering what you once were without Christ, and by realizing what you have now that you are in Him, you will revitalize your love to Him.

Notes

1. Charles Haddon Spurgeon, cited in Tom Carter, *Spurgeon at His Best* (Grand Rapids, MI: Baker Books, 1988), p. 200.
2. Leon Morris, *The Cross in the New Testament* (Grand Rapids, MI: Eerdmans, 1965), p. 410.
3. Ibid.
4. Ibid, p. 405.
5. For an in-depth treatment of justification, please see my book *The Gospel According to the Apostles* (Nashville, TN: Nelson Books, 1993, 2000).

THE PERFECT
SACRIFICE

In a small village somewhere in England there once stood a chapel, and over the arch beside it was written the words: "We Preach Christ Crucified." For years godly men preached there, presenting a crucified Savior as the only means of salvation.

As that generation of godly preachers passed on, there arose a different generation who considered the cross and its message too antiquated. So they began preaching salvation by Christ's example rather than by His blood, ignoring the necessity of His sacrifice. Meanwhile, ivy had crept up the side of the arch and covered the word *crucified,* the arch now reading, "We Preach Christ." And they did preach Him, but not as having been crucified.

Eventually people in the congregation began to question the practice of confining the sermons to Christ and the Bible. So the preachers began to give discourses on such topics as social issues, politics, philosophy, and moral rearmament. The ivy continued to grow until it wiped out the third word, rendering the phrase simply, "We Preach."

The apostle Paul wrote to the cultured Corinthians, saying, "I determined to know nothing among you except Jesus Christ, and Him crucified" (1 Cor. 2:2). The only hope of men is indeed Christ crucified, and that is the theme of Hebrews 10:1-18, the primary passage that we will examine in this chapter. In the previous chapter we analyzed Christ's substitutionary death on the cross and what it accomplished from a legal standpoint. We learned that salvation from judgment demands the substitution of a death. In this chapter we'll see that Jesus' sacrifice was superior to any offered in the Old Testament system. His death became the great and final sacrifice that accomplished for eternity what all the other sacrifices couldn't.

Christians today can easily become complacent in their love of Christ when they are continually exposed to a society that is only too eager to tolerate and excuse any sin. When churches reinforce that attitude by their own unwillingness to expose and deal with sin in either their congregation or leadership, believers will stagnate in their zeal for Christ. Why should they work hard at building their relationship with Him when they sense no urgent need to do so?

In stark contrast, the people who lived under the Old Covenant were continually exposed to a religious system that exacerbated their lack of a vital, dynamic relationship with the living God. To understand how crucial Christ's sacrifice was for you and what it accomplished, you need to first gain some insight into what it was like to live under the Mosaic Law.

The Ineffectiveness of the Old Sacrifices

Under the Old Covenant, the priests remained busy from dawn to sunset slaughtering and sacrificing animals. Particularly at Passover many thousands were slain in a week. But no matter how many sacrifices were made, or how often, they were ineffective individually and collectively. They failed in three ways: (1) They were unable to give anyone access to God, (2) they could not remove sin, and (3) they were only external.

They Couldn't Provide Access to God

The great cry in the hearts of the Old Testament saints was to be in the presence of God (see Exod. 33:15). Yet all the old ceremonies and sacrifices, though offered continually, could never save, never "make perfect those who draw near" (Heb. 10:1).

That's because the law was only "a shadow of the good things to come and not the very form" (v. 1). The law and its ceremonies could only reflect the very form of the good things to come: the privileges and blessings that would result from the sacrifice of Christ. They were form without substance. Christ's sacrifice, however, is the "very form" (*eikon*)—the exact replica or reproduction of "the good things to come." He brought forgiveness, peace, a clear conscience, and most significantly, access to God.

The good things foreshadowed and implied in the old system came to pass in Christ. The purpose of the law was never "to make perfect"—to bring to completion the salvation the people desired. But God did have some important goals for the law.

First, as a shadow, it pointed the people toward the coming reality of salvation. Peter says, "As to this salvation, the prophets who prophesied of the grace that would come to you made careful searches and inquiries" (1 Pet. 1:10). Although only a shadow, it was better than nothing because it directed the people toward God and the salvation to come.

Second, it served as a reminder that the penalty of sin is death. They couldn't avoid it: the continual slaughtering of animals as sacrifices for sin was a permanent occurrence.

Third, God gave His people the sacrifices as a covering for sin. When properly offered from a true heart of faith, the old sacrifices removed immediate, temporal judgment from God. The old sacrifices did not actually remove sin itself; they only covered it. To despise the sacrifices was to be "cut off from among his people" (Lev. 17:4) and incur God's temporal punishment, because that attitude betrayed an unbelieving, disobedient heart.

So the sacrifices, while unable to bring a person into God's presence, were important in maintaining a demonstration of a person's covenantal relationship to Him.

They Couldn't Remove Sin

The people who lived under the Mosaic Law sought deliverance from the sin and guilt that ate away at their consciences. But their sacrifices couldn't deliver them from it. In fact, the sacrifices served as a constant reminder that they couldn't. That's what the writer of Hebrews points out: "Would they not have ceased to be offered, because the worshipers, having once been cleansed, would no longer have had consciousness of sins?" But in those sacrifices there is a reminder of sins year by year (Heb. 10:2-3).

If the sacrifices had really done their job in removing sin, the people wouldn't have been burdened by its guilt. Their consciences were never cleansed as in Christ (see 9:9,14). If at any time the sacrificial system actually removed their guilt and brought them into fellowship with God, it would have ceased to be necessary because it would have accomplished its perfect end. But it never did—it just reminded them that it was ineffective for removing sin.

Imagine how burdensome living under a system like that must have been. Instead of being able to offer the sacrifice and reap forgiveness, they were constantly aware that their next sin required yet another sacrifice, which in turn was powerless to remove the sin, and to purify and free their consciences from the guilt of that sin.

How wonderful it is to know that there is no condemnation for those who are in Christ (see Rom. 8:1). It is a wonderful thing to be free from guilt and to recognize that our sins are continually being forgiven by the grace of God through the death of Christ. Our consciences are cleansed!

But there was no such freedom of conscience under the previous covenant. In fact, the more faithful and godly the person, the guiltier he was likely to feel, because he was more aware of and sensitive to God's holiness and his own sinfulness. He was torn between his knowledge of God's law and his awareness of his own breaking of that law.

That's not to say the believer is not aware of or sensitive to his own sin. No one should be more aware of it than the Christian, because, just as the faithful and godly Old Testament saint, he is more aware of God's holiness and standard of righteousness. So while he should be aware of his sin, he need not be unduly burdened with it. The forgiven sinner knows he is forgiven in Christ and is thereby delivered from fear of judgment.

They Were Only External

While sin is manifested outwardly, its root is always internal. That is an unreachable area for the old sacrifices—they could not go in-side a person and change him: "It is impossible for the blood of bulls and goats to take away sins" (Heb. 10:4). Hebrews 9:13-14 clarifies for us what was necessary to transform men: "If the blood of goats and bulls and the ashes of a heifer sprinkling those who have been defiled sanctify for the cleansing of the flesh, how much more will the blood of Christ, who through the eternal Spirit offered Himself without blemish to God, cleanse your conscience from dead works to serve the living God." There was no real relationship between the death of an animal and the forgiveness of man's moral offense against God. It was impossible for any animal to satisfy the demands of the holy God. Only Jesus Christ, the perfect union of humanity and Deity, could satisfy God and purify man. Only His death could be the ultimate, effective sacrifice.

The Effectiveness of Christ's Sacrifice

In contrast to the ineffectiveness of the animal sacrifices, Christ's sacrifice was effective for several reasons.

It Fulfilled God's Design

As we noted in the second chapter, in eternity past God the Father made a covenant with God the Son in which He would give the Son a unique gift in the form of a redeemed humanity, who would forever praise and glorify Him. To effect this promise, however, God could redeem fallen humanity only by sending His Son to earth to die. Christ's part in God's plan was to be the sacrifice that would accomplish atonement for sin. Hebrews 10:5 says, "When He comes into the world, He says, 'Sacrifice and offering You have not desired, but a body You have prepared for Me.'" When Christ was ready to be incarnated, He acknowledged the inadequacy of the old system and that His own body was to be the sacrifice that would please God and redeem back all the sinners who were a part of the covenant.

On the cross Christ ratified the eternal covenant. He did that which was necessary to provide the redemption the Father planned from before the foundation of the world.

No matter what the Father asked of Him, Christ was always prepared to accomplish His Father's will. In response to the Father's plan, He said, "I have come (in the scroll of the book it is written of Me) to do Your will, O God" (Heb. 10:7). Christ became the perfect sacrifice because He offered Himself in perfect obedience, thus fulfilling God's ultimate will.

It Replaced the Old System

The sacrifice of Jesus Christ eliminated the old system and replaced it with a new one. The writer says, "After saying above, 'Sacrifices and offerings and whole burnt offerings and sacrifices for sin You have not desired, nor have You taken pleasure in them,' (which are offered according to the Law), then He said, 'Behold, I have come to do Your will.' He takes away the first in order to establish the second" (Heb. 10:8-9). The writer's point was to show his Jewish readers that the Old Covenant was not then, never had been, and never could have been satisfactory. He sees God's displeasure with the old and His preparation of Christ as evidence that He planned to take "away the first, that He may establish the second." God's focus all along was always on the second covenant. Whatever purpose and validity the first one had, God had now set aside.

It Sanctifies the Believer

We've already seen that the old system could not make anyone holy, so God had to establish a system that could: "By this will we have been sanctified through the offering of the body of Jesus Christ once for all" (Heb. 10:10). To be sanctified, or made holy, basically means to be set apart from sin. In the context of verse 10 it refers to salvation.

The construction of the words "we are sanctified" in the Greek text is a perfect participle with a finite verb, showing in the strongest way the permanent and continuous state of salvation in which the believer exists. That means each believer has been permanently made holy. One act, in one moment, provided permanent sanctification for everyone who places his trust in Christ. On the cross He sanctified us and set us apart unto Himself.

Our experience, however, teaches us a different reality. It is difficult to think of ourselves as holy because we constantly are having to deal with sin. In thought and practice we are far from holy, but in the new nature we are perfectly holy: "In Him [we] have been made complete" (Col. 2:10). We may not always act holy, but we are holy in standing before God, just as a child who does not obey his father remains his father's child.

We are holy in the sense that before God the righteousness of Christ has been applied and imputed on our behalf. Our holiness is an accomplished fact—we have been sanctified. Regardless of how holy our walk may be, in our *standing* we are completely and permanently set apart unto God if we have trusted in "the offering of the body of Jesus Christ once for all" (Heb. 10:10).

It Removes Sin

What the other covenant couldn't do—remove sin—the New Covenant in Christ could: "Every priest stands daily ministering and offering time after time the same sacrifices, which can never take away sins; but He, having offered one sacrifice for sins for all time, sat down at the right hand of God" (Heb. 10:11-12).

The Levitical priesthood consisted of 24 orders, and in each of those orders hundreds of priests took turns serving at the altar. According to verse 11, the priests always stood while offering the sacrifices because their work was never complete. And their service of these continual sacrifices occupied them daily. In spite of their numbers and their ongoing efforts, not one of them could make an effective sacrifice for sin.

You would assume that if any member of the priesthood could make an effective offering for sin, the high priest could. Once each year, on the Day of Atonement, he would enter the holy of holies to make a sacrifice on behalf of his people. On that occasion he would sprinkle blood on the mercy seat, symbolizing the payment of the penalty for his own sins and the sins of the people. But that yearly act, although divinely prescribed and honored, had no power to remove or pay the penalty for a single sin. It could only point to the "merciful and faithful high priest" who would "make propitiation for the sins of the people" (2:17).

"Propitiation" carries the basic idea of appeasement, or satisfaction. Jesus Christ was the one Priest whose sacrifice was perfectly and permanently effective in appeasing the wrath of God because He paid the penalty for sin "by the sacrifice of Himself" (9:26). He was "offered once to bear the sins of many" (v. 28). He then "sat down at the right hand of God" (10:12) because He completed His sacrifice, having removed the sins of believers for all time.

Some things can never be reproduced, and the sacrifice of Christ is certainly one of them. It's possible, for example, to reproduce poor art, or even poor music. But if someone were to ask you to duplicate a Rembrandt, write a symphony like Beethoven or a fugue like Bach, or to write blank verse like Shakespeare or the hexameters of Homer's *Iliad,* you couldn't do it. They are masterpieces, and as such stand alone—and those are just examples from the human realm. Beyond those examples, the sacrifice of Christ is the masterpiece of the ages. It cannot be reproduced or repeated, nor should it be, for it removed sins once for all on behalf of those who believe.

It Destroyed His Enemies

All the sacrifices of the Old Testament were unable to deal with Satan. They had absolutely no effect on him at all, nor on the demons and godless men who served him. But when Jesus died on the cross, He dealt a deathblow to all His enemies. First, the cross guaranteed the ultimate destruction of "him who had the power of death, that is, the devil" (Heb. 2:14). The only way to destroy Satan was to rob him of his weapon, which was death—physical, spiritual and eternal death. And Christ did so through His own death and His ultimate resurrection, thus proving He had conquered death.

In addition to dealing with Satan, Christ also triumphed over all the other fallen angels, and He disarmed and triumphed over all rulers and authorities of all ages who have rejected and opposed God (see Col. 2:14-15). He is now only waiting until all "His enemies be made a footstool" (Heb. 10:13)—until they acknowledge His lordship by bowing at His feet (see Phil. 2:10).

All the enemies of God throughout all the ages gathered their strength together, and the best they could do was cause His physical death on a cross. Yet it was on that very cross that Christ won the victory over them. Their instrument of death became Christ's symbol of triumph over death. He conquered death for all who ever have and ever will believe in God. Jesus Christ turned Satan's worst into God's best.

It Perfected Forever the Saints

The author of Hebrews says, "By one offering He has perfected for all time those who are sanctified" (10:14). By one offering Christ brought us into God's presence forever. Consistent with the context of the verse, "perfected" refers to our eternal salvation. We can be secure in the fact that His death removes sin forever for those who belong to Him.

Of course, we need continual cleansing when we fall into sin, but we need never fear that our sin will bring about God's judgment on us. As far as Christ's sacrifice is concerned, it sufficed to sanctify and perfect us permanently and provide ongoing forgiveness. That's why He had to sacrifice Himself only once. The writer of Hebrews clarifies this truth for us when he says, "Where there is forgiveness of these things, there is no longer any offering for sin" (v. 18).

It Fulfills the Promise of a New Covenant

God had promised to bring about a New Covenant, and when Jesus died, that New Covenant was sealed with His blood. By quoting the prophecy of the New Covenant from Jeremiah 31, the writer clearly reveals God's intention. Using the testimony of the Holy Spirit Himself, the writer says, "The Holy Spirit also testifies to us; for after saying, 'This is the covenant that I will make with them after those days, says the Lord: I will put My laws upon their heart, and on their mind I will write them,' He then says, 'And their sins and their lawless deeds I will remember no more'" (Heb. 10:15-17). Jeremiah prophesied that the New Covenant would deal with man internally, making it possible for sin to be forgiven and washed away. The new sacrifice was effective because it had to accomplish the things God had promised because His promises can never be broken.

The writer concludes by saying, "Where there is forgiveness of these things, there is no longer any offering for sin" (v. 18). The work of sacrifice is finished. Forgiveness is already provided for those who trust in Christ's one perfect sacrifice. We can be thankful that we live on this side of the cross, in the glories of that perfect sacrifice, not needing to look forward to something we cannot quite see but able to look back to that which is crystal clear.

Theologian Benjamin B. Warfield appropriately sums up what the sacrifice of Christ means for Christianity:

> Not only is the doctrine of the sacrificial death of Christ embodied in Christianity as an essential element of the system, but in a very real sense it constitutes Christianity. It is this which differentiates Christianity from other religions. Christianity did not come into the world to proclaim a new morality and, sweeping away all the supernatural props by which men were wont to support their trembling, guilt-stricken souls, to throw them back on their own strong right arms to conquer a standing before God for themselves. It came to proclaim the real sacrifice for sin which God had provided in order to supersede all the poor fumbling efforts which men had made and were making to provide a sacrifice for sin for themselves; and, planting men's feet on this, to bid them go forward. It was in this sign that Christianity conquered, and it is in this sign alone that it continues to conquer.[1]

In summary, let me remind you of what Christ has done for you: The God and Sustainer of the universe humiliated Himself to become a man, suffered by hanging on a cross, and satisfied God's justice by taking man's punishment on Himself, dying in his place, and offering Himself as the one, final, perfect sacrifice. How can you ignore your relationship with the One who did all that for you? Yet many of you do whenever you give someone or something a higher priority in your life. Don't let that happen—give Him first place in your life and learn to view everything from His perspective.

Note

1. Benjamin B. Warfield, *The Works of Benjamin B. Warfield: Biblical Doctrines*, vol. 2 (New York: Oxford University Press, 1929), p. 435.

PART THREE

JESUS OUR LORD

THE NAME ABOVE ALL NAMES

Much as a drowning man searches for a hand that will grasp his and pull him to safety, man longs for eternal life. That illustration was made real to me when Tom, a man who serves in ministry with me, related the story of his own near drowning. When he was a high school senior, Tom and several friends from his church group were on a canoe trip down the Blackwater River in Florida. Rain had fallen earlier in the day, and as a result, the river was higher than normal and was running swiftly.

During one of their stops, he and two friends spotted a tire swing hanging from a tree on the opposite shore, and they decided to swim over to it. After several minutes of swinging and jumping in the river, Tom realized his legs were very tired, almost as if they were weighed down with lead. The fact that he was wearing jeans didn't help. Since he was unable to continue treading water, he sank like a rock to the bottom, which was about 8 to 10 feet below the surface. As soon as he reached the riverbed, he pushed off against it and rose back up to the surface. He called out to his friend nearest him on the shore, saying he could use some help. His friend, thinking Tom was only kidding, ignored him. As the current carried him farther downstream, Tom sank again. He pushed off the bottom once again, but this time he was barely able to break the surface, getting his head just far enough out of the water to cry out for help.

Tom's friend, now realizing the severity of Tom's predicament, began running along the bank to get ahead of Tom. He found a tree limb angling out over the river, and grabbed hold with one arm. With his other he stretched as far as he could. Meanwhile, Tom had gone under a third time. When he pushed off the bottom this time, he realized he was not going to make it to the surface. As he rose up to within a few inches of the surface, he saw through the shimmering water the outline of a hand stretching out toward him. He reached for that hand with his own and managed to grab it! Immediately he flexed all the muscles in his arm and, with the strength of his friend, was pulled out of the water. His friend was able to secure a strong hold on Tom until the rest of their party could get to them.

Tom was fortunate—his friend happened to be in the right position and had the power to save him. Apart from him, Tom would have drowned that day. When it comes to spiritual rescue from judgment and hell, our Savior was able and eager to reach out to us and save us from eternal death. He assures us, "Because I live, you will live also" (John 14:19).

Our risen Lord and Savior has given His brethren (those who trust and believe in His ability to save them) the greatest gift of all—eternal *life*. How any believer, then, could neglect or ignore his relationship to Christ is beyond comprehension. Yet many Christians do, allowing their self-centeredness and the enticements of the world to distract and dominate their thinking so that they turn from looking to Christ, leaving their first love. All believers would do well—both those who need to return to their first love and those who still love Him with the devotion of their heart, soul, mind and strength—to recall how God rewarded His Son because of His willingness to die for sinners.

In the previous chapters we considered the humiliation of Christ—how He fulfilled God's plan to save man. He who existed in the form of God "did not regard equality with God a thing to be grasped, but emptied Himself, taking the form of a bondservant, and being made in the likeness of men. Being found in appearance as a man, He humbled Himself by becoming obedient to the point of death, even death on a cross" (Phil. 2:6-8). In so doing, Jesus became the perfect substitute and sacrifice—He died in our place, took our sins on His sinless frame, and reconciled us to God by appeasing God's wrath.

Yet if Christ's work on the cross ended with His death and was a noble martyrdom only, we would be drowning men and women, with no one nearby to reach out to pull us to safety. However sacrificial His death was, a dead Savior couldn't deliver sinners because that would mean He was unable to conquer the penalty of sin—death. But Jesus Christ did defeat death and rose again. For that very reason "God highly exalted Him, and bestowed on Him the name which is above every name, so that at the name of Jesus every knee will bow, of those who are in heaven and on earth and under the earth, and that every tongue will confess that Jesus Christ is Lord, to the glory of God the Father" (vv. 9-11).

So then, the gospel is not complete without the exaltation of Jesus Christ. In this text, which is likely a hymn of the early church, we see our Lord descending from His glory as God to take on the form of a servant, dying, rising, and then ascending and returning to the glory He had with the Father before the world began. That is the complete Christian message. The humiliation and death of Jesus was only the first phase. In this chapter we'll look at the next stage in the unfolding of God's plan for the incarnate Lord and discover how our Savior regained the glory He had with the Father before the world existed (see John 17:5). It is my sincere hope that in seeing your exalted Lord, you will realize how much He deserves your complete and undivided love and loyalty.

The Steps of His Exaltation

In chapter 3 we examined the apostle Paul's record of the series of steps our Savior took in His descent to become a man: He chose not to use many of His divine prerogatives, humbled Himself, became a servant, identified with sinners, looked like a man, and was obedient to the point of death on a cross (see Phil. 2:5-8). Although Paul doesn't treat God's exaltation of Christ in the same manner, Scripture as a whole attests to several steps that do comprise and complete His exaltation: His resurrection, ascension, coronation, and present intercession.

His Resurrection

The resurrection of Jesus Christ is without question the pinnacle of redemptive history. It proves beyond a doubt the deity of Jesus Christ and guarantees our own resurrection. Most important, it is the crowning proof that God accepted the sacrifice of Jesus Christ, "who was delivered up because of our transgressions, and was raised because of our justification" (Rom. 4:25). Paul's imagery in that verse pictures a criminal being remanded to his punishment. In a similar manner Jesus Christ was delivered up as our Substitute to serve the sentence of death our transgressions deserved. But He was also raised up to provide the justification before God that we could never attain on our own. The great nineteenth-century theologian Charles Hodge wrote:

> With a dead Saviour, a Saviour over whom death had triumphed and held captive, our justification had been forever impossible. As it was necessary that the high priest, under the old economy, should not only slay the victim at the altar, but carry the blood into the most holy place, and sprinkle it upon the mercy-seat; so it was necessary not only that our great High Priest should suffer in the outer court, but that He should pass into heaven to present his righteousness before God for our justification. Both, therefore, as the evidence of the acceptance of his satisfaction on our behalf, and as a necessary step to secure the application of the merits of his sacrifice, the resurrection of Christ was absolutely essential, even for our justification.[1]

The fact is, "if Christ has not been raised, your faith is worthless; you are still in your sins" (1 Cor. 15:17). If Jesus did not rise from the dead, then sin won the victory over Christ and therefore continues to be victorious over us all. If Jesus remained dead, then when we die, we too will remain dead and damned to eternal punishment. If Christ did not defeat death, His death was useless, our faith in Him is useless, and God still holds our sins against us. If Christ was not raised by God, then He did not reconcile us to God, redeem us from the penalty of our sin, bring about the forgiveness of sins, and provide the one and perfect sacrifice for sins. If all of those things were true, then His death would be nothing more than the heroic death of a noble martyr, the pathetic death of a madman, or the execution of a fraud. All men would be damned and eternal heaven empty of all but God and holy angels.

But God *did* raise Jesus from the dead (see Rom. 4:25). His death *did* pay the price for our sins, and His resurrection proved it. When God raised Jesus from the dead, He demonstrated that His Son had offered the full satisfaction for sin that the law demands.

Not only that, Christ's resurrection proves His power over the supreme penalty of sin—death. The grave could not hold Jesus because He had conquered death, and His conquest over death bequeaths eternal life to every person who trusts in Him. The apostle Peter said, "God raised Him up again, putting an end to the agony of death, since it was impossible for Him to be held in its power" (Acts 2:24).

Death was powerless to hold Jesus for several reasons. First, death could not contain Him because He possessed divine power. Jesus was "the resurrection and the life" (John 11:25) who died "that through death He might render powerless him who had the power of death, that is, the devil" (Heb. 2:14). Satan's power to kill us had to be broken for us to be brought to God, so in His resurrection, our Lord robbed Satan of his supreme strategy. Death is a powerful satanic weapon, but God has a weapon that is more powerful—eternal life—and with it Jesus destroyed death. The way to eternal life is through resurrection, so Jesus went into death, through death, and came out the other side.

Divine promise was a second reason that death was not able to hold Jesus. John 2:18-22 records the following dialogue:

The Jews then said to Him, "What sign do You show us as your authority for doing these things?" Jesus answered them, "Destroy this temple, and in three days I will raise it up." The Jews then said, "It took forty-six years to build this temple, and will You raise it up in three days?" But He was speaking of the temple of His body. So when He was raised from the dead, His disciples remembered that He said this; and they believed the Scripture and the word which Jesus had spoken.

"Thus it is written," our Lord told the disciples, "that the Christ would suffer and rise again from the dead the third day" (Luke 24:46). Jesus Himself, who is the Truth, the incarnate God who cannot lie, promised that He would rise from the dead.

Third, death could not hold Him because of divine purpose. God planned that His people be with Him for all eternity. But to be with Him, they needed to go through death and out the other side, and Jesus had to blaze the trail (see 1 Cor. 15:16-26). He promised the Father He would raise all God's people up and lose none of them, but bring them to heaven (see John 6:37-40).

So, by demonstrating His ability to conquer death—a power belonging only to God Himself (the Giver of life)—Christ established beyond all doubt that He was God the Son (see Rom. 1:4). Thus the Resurrection is proof that Christ's sacrifice was acceptable to God to atone for sins, and as God, He had the power to conquer death and raise the dead. Theologian Benjamin B. Warfield comments:

> That He died manifests His love and His willingness to save. It is His rising again that manifests His power and His ability to save. We cannot be saved by a dead Christ, who undertook but could not perform, and who still lies under the Syrian sky, another martyr of impotent love. To save, He must pass not merely to but through death. If the penalty was fully paid, it cannot have broken Him, it must needs have been broken upon Him. The resurrection of Christ is thus the indispensable evidence of His completed work, of His accomplished redemption. It is only because He rose from the dead that we know that the ran-

som He offered was sufficient, the sacrifice was accepted, and that we are His purchased possession. In one word, the resurrection of Christ is fundamental to the Christian hope and the Christian confidence.[2]

His Ascension

Acts 1:9-11 describes the second aspect of Christ's exaltation. After Christ finished His final instructions to His disciples, "He was lifted up while they were looking on, and a cloud received Him out of their sight. And as they were gazing intently into the sky while He was going, behold, two men in white clothing stood beside them. They also said, 'Men of Galilee, why do you stand looking into the sky? This Jesus, who has been taken up from you into heaven, will come in just the same way as you have watched Him go into heaven.'" Without fanfare, Jesus, in His glorious resurrection body, left this world for the realm of heaven to take His rightful place on the Father's throne at His right hand.

His Coronation

After God raised Jesus from the dead and He ascended into heaven, Paul says God "seated Him at His right hand in the heavenly places, far above all rule and authority and power and dominion, and every name that is named, not only in this age, but also in the one to come. And He put all things in subjection under His feet" (Eph. 1:20-22). The writer of Hebrews affirms the same truth: "When He had made purification of sins, He sat down at the right hand of the Majesty on high" (Heb. 1:3). Jesus' sitting down at His Father's right hand signifies at least four things.

First, He sat down as a sign of honor, "that every tongue will confess that Jesus Christ is Lord, to the glory of God the Father" (Phil. 2:11). To be seated at the right hand of the Father is the highest honor.

Second, He sat down as a sign of authority. Peter declared that Christ "is at the right hand of God, having gone into heaven, after angels and authorities and powers had been subjected to Him" (1 Pet. 3:22). Throughout the Old and New Testaments, the right hand is a symbol of preeminence, power and authority. At the right hand of God Christ acts with the authority and the power of Almighty God over all created things. That's where Jesus went when He had accomplished His work on the cross, and that's where He rules from today. Matthew 28:18 records Jesus' affirmation of His authority: "All authority has been given to Me in heaven and on earth." Even all judgment was given to Him (see John 5:27). Christ sat down as the sovereign of the universe.

Third, He sat down to rest. There were no seats in the tabernacle or the temple sanctuaries because the Old Covenant priests offered sacrifices continually throughout the day—their work was never done. But Jesus, the perfect High Priest, sat down because His work was complete: "But He, having offered one sacrifice for sins for all time, sat down at the right hand of God" (Heb. 10:12).

The fourth and final reason He sat down relates directly with the final stage of Christ's exaltation: He sat down to intercede for His people.

His Intercession
Jesus Christ is our High Priest, who sat down to plead before God's throne for us. In Romans 8:34 Paul shows the progress of Christ's exaltation: "Christ Jesus is He who died, yes, rather who was raised, who is at the right hand of God, who also intercedes for us." Our Lord is seated at God's right hand at this moment, making intercession for all of us who belong to Him. (We'll leave these truths for now but will examine in-depth this vital ministry of Christ in the next chapter.)

When Jesus came into the world, He entered a state of being He had never before experienced, the condition of humiliation. Commentator William Hendricksen reminds us that He was restored to glory and exaltation:

> The exaltation is the reversal of humiliation. He who stood condemned in relation to the divine law (because of the sin of the world which rested on Him) has exchanged this penalty for the righteous relation to the law. He who was

poor has become rich. He who was rejected has been accepted (Rev. 12:5,10). He who learned obedience has entered upon the actual administration of the power and authority committed to Him.

As *king*, having by His death, resurrection, and ascension achieved and displayed His triumph over His enemies, He now holds in His hands the reins of the universe, and rules all things in the interest of His church (Eph. 1:22, 23). As *prophet* He through His Spirit leads His own in all the truth. And as *priest* (High-priest according to the order of Melchizedek) He, on the basis of His accomplished atonement, *not only intercedes but actually lives forever to make intercession* for those who draw near to God through Him.[3]

Wonderfully, all believers will follow Christ in His exaltation. We will enter into His eternal glory. We will also ascend—not just believers alive at the time of the Rapture, but also all the dead in Christ. In heaven we will experience coronation, for we will sit with Christ on His throne (see Rev. 3:21). No longer will we need our Lord's intercessory ministry, because our transformation will be complete. The path of glory Jesus followed beginning with His resurrection is the path we will follow as well. That's God's promise.

At no time in His exaltation did Jesus neglect or ignore you; He paved the way to heaven for you. He anchored your salvation within the veil in the heavenly holy of holies (see Heb. 6:19-20). Don't ever lose sight of that truth. Look to your first love—your exalted Lord—and revel in your coming glory.

A New Name

According to Philippians 2:9, when "God highly exalted Him . . . [He] bestowed on Him the name which is above every name." Since Paul used the definite article before "name," we have to ask what is *the* name that is above every name? Hebrews 1:4 says this name is more excellent than the angels' names. It has to be a name that goes beyond merely distinguishing one person from another; it must be a name that is descriptive of Christ's nature—revealing something of His essential being. It has to be a superlative name—one that would set Christ beyond all others and above all comparison.

The only name mentioned in Philippians 2:9-11 that could satisfy such requirements is "Lord." In verse 11 Paul says, "Every tongue will confess that Jesus Christ is Lord." "Lord" is the name that is above every name because whoever is Lord is the supreme One. "Jesus" is His name of humiliation. "Christ" is a title. "Lord" is His name of exaltation.

The Gospels clearly show that "Lord" was to be His new name: Christ acknowledged before Pilate that He was a King (see Mark 15:2; John 18:37). Thomas looked on the resurrected Christ and it was always evident that Christ was the living God and thus Lord; it was in His exaltation that He was formally given the name "Lord," the name above every name.

The Greek word translated "Lord" (*kurios*) primarily refers to the right to rule, thus its inherent meaning is not deity but rulership. *Kurios* was used in the New Testament to describe a master or owner. It was a title of respect for anyone in control and became the official title of the Roman emperors. It was used as a title for heathen deities. The translators of the Greek Old Testament used *kurios* to translate the name of God (the Hebrew word *Yahweh*). So while deity could be associated with the word, its primary meaning is rulership—secular or otherwise. To say Jesus is *kurios* certainly implies deity, but sovereign authority is the main idea. Regardless of the meaning, all must acknowledge Jesus' supremacy and right to rule.

We cannot know Christ any other way than as Lord. That's why the first creed in the history of the church, given in Philippians 2:11, says, "Jesus Christ is Lord." Paul said, "We do not preach ourselves, but Christ Jesus as Lord" (2 Cor. 4:5). Salvation comes only to those who confess Jesus as Lord (see Rom. 10:9-10). Jesus rejected the rich man who refused to obey His sovereign will and submit to Him (see Matt. 19:16-22). Every Christian must acknowledge that—it's the very substance of Christianity. Jesus is Lord and those who refuse

Him as Lord cannot call Him Savior. Everyone who truly receives Him is divinely brought to surrender to His authority.

The centrality of the lordship of Christ is very clear in the New Testament gospel. The Jesus who is Savior cannot be separated from the Jesus who is Lord, just as God cannot be separated from His authority, dominion, rulership, and right to command. As sovereign Lord, He commands and deserves our allegiance and love. Nothing less will suffice. If you call yourself a Christian, your love to Him must be your ultimate priority. "If you love Me," He said, "you will keep My commandments" (John 14:15). Obedience from the heart is the evidence of first love.

The Response to Christ's Exaltation

Only one response is appropriate to Christ's exaltation: "At the name of Jesus every knee will bow, of those who are in heaven and on earth and under the earth, and that every tongue will confess that Jesus Christ is Lord" (Phil. 2:10-11). As our Lord, Jesus Christ deserves our worship. God exalted Him and gave Him the name "Lord" to affirm His authority and cause everyone to bow to Him.

Acknowledge Him as God
Philippians 2:10 says that at His name, Lord, we are to bow. The subjunctive mood here ("every knee will bow") says that every knee eventually *will* bow—either by choice or by force. By God's grace some are enabled to acknowledge Christ's lordship by choice. Others will bow to Him by force of divine judgment. The phrases "every knee will bow" (v. 10) and "every tongue will confess" (v. 11) are taken from Isaiah 45:23, which strongly emphasizes the sole authority and sovereignty of God. In context the Lord said:

> There is no other God besides Me, a righteous God and a Savior; there is none except Me. Turn to Me and be saved, all the ends of the earth; for I am God, and there is no other. I have sworn by Myself, the word has gone forth from My mouth in righteousness and will not turn back,

that to Me every knee will bow, every tongue will swear allegiance. They will say of Me, "Only in the Lord are righteousness and strength" (45:21-24).

To whom would you liken Me and make Me equal and compare Me, that we would be alike? Those who lavish gold from the purse and weigh silver on the scale hire a goldsmith, and he makes it into a god; they bow down, indeed they worship it. They lift it upon the shoulder and carry it; they set it in its place and it stands there. It does not move from its place. Though one may cry to it, it cannot answer; it cannot deliver him from his distress. Remember this, and be assured; recall it to mind, you transgressors. Remember the former things long past, for I am God, and there is no other; I am God, and there is no one like Me, declaring the end from the beginning, and from ancient times things which have not been done, saying, "My purpose will be established, and I will accomplish all My good pleasure" (46:5-10).

Isaiah 45–46 clearly establishes that God is Lord and sovereign. Paul is saying that what is true of God is true of the Lord Jesus Christ—every knee will bow and every tongue will confess that He is Lord of all. We know Him as the Lord, and we know Him as Jesus (the name associated with His saving work; see Matt. 1:21). But He must be known as both to be known at all. One receives the gift of salvation by receiving Jesus, the humiliated Savior, and bowing the knee to Him as majestic, sovereign Lord.

Those Who Will Acknowledge Him as Lord

Philippians 2:10 affirms that the entire intelligent universe is called to worship Christ: "Those who are in heaven and on earth and under the earth."

Those in Heaven

The heavenly group consists of the angels and men. They already acknowledge that Jesus is Lord. The angelic group consists of God's holy, elect angels—the unfallen seraphim, cherubim, and myriads of other angels who worship God in heaven. The spirits of redeemed believers are the triumphant Old Testament and New Testament saints now in the presence of Christ: "the general assembly and church of the firstborn who are enrolled in heaven . . . the spirits of the righteous made perfect" (Heb. 12:23).

Those on Earth

The earthly group is made up of both believers and unbelievers still alive. As believers we submit to Christ as Lord and Savior, having followed the pattern of Romans 10:9: "If you confess with your mouth Jesus as Lord, and believe in your heart that God raised Him from the dead, you will be saved."

The disobedient on earth will also bow before Jesus Christ, but by compulsion. Second Thessalonians 1:7-9 says, "When the Lord Jesus shall be revealed from heaven with His mighty angels in flaming fire, [He will deal out retribution] to those who do not know God and to those who do not obey the gospel of our Lord Jesus. These will pay the penalty of eternal destruction, away from the presence of the Lord and from the glory of His power." When Jesus returns to subdue the earth, He will remove the wicked from the earth, cast them into hell, and establish His kingdom.

Those Under the Earth

"Under the earth" refers to the place of eternal punishment, which is occupied by demons and evil men. They too will acknowledge the lordship of Christ—not by enjoying His reign, but by bearing the unending expression of His wrath in eternal torment.

Jesus Christ is Lord everywhere in the universe. Therefore "every tongue will confess that Jesus Christ is Lord" (Phil. 2:11). To *confess* means "to acknowledge," "affirm" or "agree." Everyone—demons, men, holy angels, glorified saints—will acknowledge His lordship. History is moving toward the day when Jesus will be acknowledged by all as the supreme ruler of the universe. He already sits in the seat of power, but has not yet brought the fallen universe fully under His authority. We live in days of grace, during which He brings men and women to acknowledge Him as Lord willingly rather than by force. But one day He will subdue everything in the universe: "When all things are subjected to Him, then the Son Himself also will be subjected to the One who subjected all things to Him, that God may be all in all" (1 Cor. 15:28). God is glorified in anything that lifts up or exalts the Son. That's what Paul was referring to when he said that when all acknowledge that Jesus Christ is Lord, it redounds "to the glory of God the Father" (Phil. 2:11).

That Jesus is Lord is the most important confession of Christianity. He is to be confessed as Lord by one's mouth and in one's heart. Does He continually have the preeminence in your life? D. Martyn Lloyd-Jones asks:

> What is Jesus Christ to us? Where does He come into our scheme of things? What do we believe concerning Him? Have we bowed the knee to Him, have we surrendered to Him, do we make this confession concerning Him? Do we say that Jesus of Nazareth, that man who walked about the face of this earth, is Lord, the anointed of God, the One who was set apart to bear the sins of man, including our own? Do we say that it is there alone, in that death, that we find salvation and all that it means, and by which we are reconciled to God? Do we confess that to us He is God and that we worship Him to the glory of God? . . .
>
> How easy it is to turn the New Testament into a philosophy or a set of rules and regulations and a scheme for life and living, a general outlook . . . I do not accept the Christian philosophy primarily; I accept *Him.* I believe on Him, I bow my knee to Him, the Person. I make a statement about the individual; Jesus Christ is Lord, He is my Lord; it is a personal relationship, and a personal confession.[4]

Because He is the exalted Lord, He gives us the assurance that our redemption is complete and our hope of heaven is secure. We also can be assured that He continually intercedes on our behalf with the Father. A gospel that stops with the humiliation of Christ is incomplete. He must be seen as the resurrected, ascended, crowned and interceding Christ. Of those truths, Benjamin B. Warfield wrote:

> In the resurrection of Christ, we have the assurance that He is the Lord of heaven and earth whose right it is to rule and in whose hands are gathered the reins of the universe. . . . Had He not risen, could we believe Him enthroned in heaven, Lord of all? Himself subject to death; Himself the helpless prisoner of the grave; does He differ in kind from that endless procession of the slaves of death journeying like Him through the world to the one inevitable end? If it is fundamental to Christianity that Jesus should be Lord of *all*; that God should have highly exalted Him and given Him the name which is above *every* name; that in the name of Jesus *every* knee should bow, and *every* tongue confess Him as Lord: then it is fundamental to Christianity that death too should be subject to Him and it should not be possible for Him to see corruption. This last enemy too He must needs, as Paul asserts, put under His feet; and it is because He has put this last enemy under His feet that we can say with such energy of conviction that nothing can separate us from the love of God which is in Christ Jesus our Lord—not even death itself: and that nothing can harm us and nothing can take away our peace.[5]

Don't ever forget that at this moment, the Lord of heaven and earth, who is your own personal Lord and Savior, waits for your fellowship and eager obedience. Having seen who He is—the exalted Lord and Savior who saved you from certain death—should prompt you to renew your commitment to love Him.

Notes
1. Charles Hodge, *Commentary on the Epistle to the Romans* (Grand Rapids, MI: Eerdmans, 1983), p. 129.
2. Benjamin B. Warfield, *The Saviour of the World* (Carlisle, PA: The Banner of Truth Trust, 1991), p. 210.
3. William Hendricksen, *Philippians, Colossians and Philemon* (Grand Rapids, MI: Baker Books, 1962), p. 11. Emphasis in original.
4. D. Martyn Lloyd-Jones, *The Life of Joy, An Exposition of Philippians 1 and 2* (Grand Rapids, MI: Baker Books, 1989), pp. 153-154.
5. Warfield, *The Savior of the World*, pp. 211-212. Emphasis in original.

AT THE RIGHT
HAND OF GOD

We live in a troubled world with an uncertain future. The fixtures of a responsible society that we once considered safe and secure are now threatened by godless, anti-Christian perspectives. While many contend that through educational achievement and intellectual prowess mankind should be on the verge of even greater cultural and social advancements, the fact is our world is increasingly skeptical and many people fear that we may be facing more vexing problems than at any time in history. Local newspapers along with the nightly news attest daily to the ruined lives left in the wake of a sinful society running wild—a society that is increasingly unthwarted by weak morals, families and governments. Tremendous technological breakthroughs may suffice to enhance world communications, improve health care, and provide the latest in creature comforts, but not one has any application to the hearts, souls, minds and morals of people who live with dissatisfaction, unfulfillment, guilt, fear, pain and sorrow at a level I have never seen in my lifetime.

That kind of attitude toward life has even found its way into the church. Without realizing it, Christians all too easily adopt a worldly mindset along with its accompanying emptiness. As a result, when they reach those inevitable hours of life that are filled with pain, confusion and trouble, they may turn their backs on divine realities and resources and listen to the siren calls of the world and pursue solutions concocted by men.

No one would argue that being a Christian in this society is easy. While we certainly don't face the overt persecution that fellow believers face in other parts of the world, we are plagued by subtler pressures. The breakdown of the family has had a profound cross-over effect on Christian families. The societal pressures that devastate secular marriages crowd their way into the church and attempt to, and sometimes do, destroy Christian marriages. Raising children in a society and an educational system that has lost virtually all respect for morality exerts a tremendous amount of stress on Christian parents. The unbelievable tension and difficulty in safeguarding children who are exposed to sinful peer pressure is unlike anything our parents had to deal with. And we're all shocked by the growing tolerance for the sort of wickedness and evil that would have engendered outright revulsion a generation ago. Our world's values are the antithesis of Christian virtue.

Satan doesn't want us to look to Christ; he wants us to depend on ourselves and the long list of man-made solutions. When we do, he attacks in two areas. First, he'll cause us to doubt God's power and view our trials and temptations as too overwhelming, even for God. Once he has us focusing on our impossible circumstances and not trusting the wisdom, power and purpose of the Lord, and has successfully diverted us from pursuing our relationship with Christ, he has led us into a more desperate condition.

Satan also assaults us by causing us to doubt God's forgiveness in our ongoing struggle with sin. While Christ's death and resurrection eradicated the penalty of sin, we have not yet escaped its presence. Daily sin attempts through the flesh to regain its dominion over us. Satan wants us to forget that "having been freed from sin, [we] became slaves of righteousness" (Rom. 6:18). Sin can seem overpowering, especially if it goes unconfessed, and Satan will use it to raise doubts about the reality of salvation in Christ, reasoning that if one were truly saved, one wouldn't struggle with sin. By bringing continual accusations, Satan, if so allowed, will deflect a believer's focus off the One who already paid the penalty for those very sins and cause him to lose heart, assurance, joy and peace.

As a Christian, you don't have to succumb to the wiles of the devil (see 1 Pet. 5:8-10). We have a living Lord who is all-powerful and there is no trial too hard for us in His strength (see 2 Cor. 10:13; Phil. 4:19). And we have a risen Savior who conquered sin and Satan for us and has all the resources necessary to resist the devil and his assaults on us. In the previous chapter we noted that the final phase of Christ's exaltation is His current ministry of intercession for Christians. It is in this very ministry, as He fulfills the roles of our sympathetic High Priest and Advocate with the Father, that our Lord in heaven comes to our aid in everything, so that we are more than conquerors (see Rom. 8:38). Jude 24 says, "Now to Him who is able to keep you from stumbling, and to make you stand in the presence of His glory blameless with great joy." And it is that very ministry that ought to motivate you, if you have forgotten all He does for you each and every day, to return to your first love.

Our Sympathetic High Priest

Christ's Perfect Sympathy

For a priest in the Old Testament to truly represent the people, he had to be "taken from among men" (Heb. 5:1). Only another man could be subject to the temptations of men, experience suffering like men, and thereby be able to represent them to God in an understanding and compassionate way. Jesus Christ could not be a true High Priest unless He were a man. In sending His Son, Jesus Christ, God entered into the human world and felt everything that men will ever feel that "He might become a merciful and faithful high priest" (2:17). Thus Jesus is our perfect priest, "For we do not have a high priest who cannot sympathize with our weaknesses, but One who has been tempted in all things as we are, yet without sin" (4:15).

When we are troubled, hurt, despondent or strongly tempted, we want to be able to share our feelings with someone who understands and who has been successful in dealing with it. Jesus *can* "sympathize with our weaknesses." He has an unequaled capacity for sympathizing with us in every danger, trial or situation that comes our way, because He's been through it all: "Since He Himself was tempted in that which He has suffered, He is able to come to the aid of those who are tempted" (2:18). When Paul speaks of "the fellowship of [Christ's] sufferings" (Phil. 3:10), he is affirming the privilege of having a partner in his pain who fully understands.

Jesus not only had all the feelings of love, concern, disappointment, grief and frustration that we have, but He also had much greater love, more sensitive concerns, infinitely higher standards of righteousness, and perfect awareness of the evil and dangers of sin. Contrary to what we are inclined to think, His divinity made His temptations and trials immeasurably harder for Him to endure than ours are for us, because He never yielded, thus feeling the full assault.

To illustrate, we can experience only so much pain before we lose consciousness or go into shock. When I was thrown out of a car that was traveling about 75 miles an hour, I slid across the highway on my back for about a hundred yards. I felt pain for a while and then I didn't feel anything. Our bodies have a way of turning off pain when it becomes too much to endure. Although people vary in their pain thresholds, we all have a breaking point. So there is a degree of pain we will never experience because our bodies will shut off our sensitivity in one way or another.

The same thing is true in temptation. There is a degree of temptation we will never experience because we succumb long before we reach that point. Since Jesus never sinned, He took the full extent of all that Satan could throw at Him. He had no weakness limit to turn off temptation at a certain point by giving in. Since He never succumbed, He experienced every temptation to the maximum. And no human has ever been perfectly holy as He was, so no human has ever had the sensitivity to sin He had. He would have felt any effort to destroy His holy perfection in its most infant subtlety. So in every way He was tempted as we are, and more. The only difference was that He never sinned. He knows everything we know, and a great deal we do not know, about temptation, testing and pain. The Greek word translated "weaknesses" (4:15) refers to all the natural limitations of humanity, including liability to sin. Jesus knew firsthand the drive of human nature toward sin. His humanity was His battleground. It is there that Jesus faced and fought sin. He was victorious, but not without the most intense temptation, grief and anguish.

Despite the intensity of His battle with sin, Jesus was "without sin." The two Greek words translated "without sin" express the complete absence of sin. Though He was relentlessly tempted to sin, not the slightest bit of sin ever entered His mind, let alone was ever expressed in His words and actions.

Some people wonder how Jesus could understand our struggle with sin since He never sinned. He knew sin very well because He knew holiness so perfectly. He knows sin better than anyone since the very fact that He never sinned demonstrates His utterly perfect awareness of any hint of it approaching. He can recognize temptation before we ever know it's present. What a High Priest we have to intercede for us in our temptations!

Jesus' righteous response to the temptation of sin qualifies Him to sympathize with us. "For consider Him who has endured such hostility by sinners against Himself, so that you will not grow weary and lose heart. You have not yet resisted to the point of shedding blood in your striving against sin" (Heb. 12:3-4). Because He knows us and our struggles intimately, Jesus leads us down the path of victory over them: "No temptation has overtaken you but such as is common to man; and God is faithful, who will not allow you to be tempted beyond what you are able, but with the temptation will provide the way of escape also, so that you will be able to endure it" (1 Cor. 10:13).

The following story is told of a man named Booth Tucker, who was conducting evangelistic meetings in the great Salvation Army Citadel in Chicago and who experienced firsthand the helping hand of Christ. One night, after Tucker had preached on the sympathy of Jesus, a man came forward and asked him how he could talk about a loving, understanding, sympathetic God. "If your wife had just died, like mine has," the man said, "and your babies were crying for their mother who would never come back, you wouldn't be saying what you're saying."

A few days later, Mr. Tucker's wife was killed in a train accident. Her body was brought to Chicago and carried to the Citadel for the funeral. After the service the bereaved preacher looked down into the silent face of his wife and then turned to those who were attending. "The other day when I was here," he said, "a man told me that, if my wife had just died and my children were crying for their mother, I would not be able to say that Christ was understanding and sympathetic, or that He was sufficient for every need. If that man is here, I want to tell him that Christ is sufficient. My heart is broken, it is crushed, but it has a song, and Christ put it there. I want to tell that man that Jesus Christ speaks comfort to me today." The man was there, and he came and knelt beside the casket while Booth Tucker introduced him to Jesus Christ.

Christ's Perfect Provision

Knowledge and sympathy for another's struggles are important, but if you don't have the resources to help someone in that struggle, your sympathy is limited. While I can pray for someone who is going through some spiritual struggle and empathize with his pain, I don't have the power or the resources to change the situation that caused the trouble. But Jesus, our High Priest, does have the resources: "Therefore let us draw near with confidence to the throne of grace, that we may receive mercy and may find grace to help in time of need" (Heb. 4:16).

The "throne of grace" is another name for God's throne. It would have been a throne of judgment if Jesus had not sprinkled His blood upon it and transformed it into a throne of grace for all who trust in Him.

There is a distinction between "receiving mercy" and "finding grace." Mercy is compassion toward our misery, and grace becomes the source of transforming power to overcome that misery. We can approach God's throne with eagerness and confidence. It is not a throne of judgment for us as it is for sinners, because Christ is there interceding on our behalf, having made atonement for our sins. It is not a throne of indifference, because Christ is a sympathetic High Priest who knows exactly what we feel. It is a throne of grace because He will dispense the grace we need for every concern of life. Regarding this fundamental truth, D. Martyn Lloyd-Jones writes:

> The object of the high priest in going into the holiest of all once a year was to obtain certain benefits for the people he represented. First and foremost was forgiveness; then, all the blessings needed from God for their daily lives, the goodwill of God and the blessings following the goodwill. Our Lord does exactly the same for us in heaven. The presence of the Lord Jesus Christ at the right hand of God is a guarantee that we can have mercy. It is now "a throne of grace" to us because He is there. So, knowing that I shall receive mercy, I can go into the presence of God with boldness, with assurance. But I not only get mercy I also get "grace to help in time of need." I get everything I need; and that, through the Lord Jesus Christ. In this way He makes intercession for me.[1]

It is in this very ministry of Christ that the truth of 1 John 4:19 is made real to us: "We love, because He first loved us." Your only hope of reinvigorating your love for Christ is to understand the depth of His love for you. For that reason alone you ought not to neglect the priority of your love for Him.

Our Advocate with the Father

One aspect of Christ's function as our High Priest in heaven is His advocacy before the Father. When Satan calls into question the reality of our salvation because of our sin, we can turn to Christ: "If we confess our sins, He is faithful and righteous to forgive us our sins and to cleanse us from all unrighteousness" (1 John 1:9) because in Him "we have an Advocate with the Father, Jesus Christ the righteous; and He Himself is the propitiation for our sins" (2:1-2).

Our Righteous Defender

When we sin, Jesus is our "advocate." That word is a translation of the Greek word *paracletos*, the same word that is translated "Comforter" in reference to the Holy Spirit (John 15:26). *Paracletos* means "a lawyer for the defense" or "someone called alongside to help."

Satan is unrelenting in his efforts to accuse believers before God. Revelation 12:10 says he is before the throne of God day and night accusing God's children. If we were to depict this scene in a courtroom setting, Satan would be the prosecutor and Christ the lawyer for our defense. But Satan has no case against us—it can never get a hearing in God's court—because our Advocate has Himself paid the penalty for our sin. The Almighty Judge has already declared us not guilty. The apostle Paul asks, "Who will bring a charge against God's elect?" after God Himself has already justified them (Rom. 8:33). Satan can't successfully accuse us because Christ has removed all our sins from the record. There is no condemnation ever to those in Christ (see Rom. 8:1).

"Jesus Christ the righteous . . . is the propitiation [appeasement] for our sins" (1 John 2:1-2). When we are accused, Jesus doesn't plead our innocence to God; rather, He pleads His own righteousness, which has been granted to us by grace through faith. God's hatred of sin had to be appeased, and Jesus Christ's death paid for our sins. Thus He satisfied God's justice.

Our Secure Salvation

Because Christ paid the penalty for sin and reconciled us to God as a result, Paul says "we have obtained our introduction by faith into this grace in which we stand" (Rom. 5:2). He has given us *permanent* access to God. That's the idea behind the word "stand" (Greek *histemi*). Although faith is necessary for salvation, it is God's grace working in the believer that generates that faith. We are not saved by divine grace and then preserved through human effort. To the Philippian believers Paul declared, "He who began a good work in you will perfect it until the day of Christ Jesus" (Phil. 1:6).

We've already established that believers will fall into sin, but their sin is not more powerful than God's grace. They are the very sins for which Jesus paid the full penalty. If no sin a person commits before salvation is too great for Christ's atoning death to cover, surely no sin he commits after salvation is too great to be covered. Paul declares, "For if while we were enemies we were reconciled to God through the death of His Son, much more, having been reconciled, we shall be saved by His life" (Rom. 5:10).

Paul means that if a dying Savior could bring us to salvation, surely a living Savior can keep us in His grace. If God had the power and the grace to redeem us in the first place, how much more does He have the power and the grace to keep us redeemed? Our Savior not only delivered us from sin and its judgment, but also delivers us from uncertainty and doubt about that deliverance. How can a Christian, whose past and future salvation are secured by God, be insecure? If sin was no barrier to the beginning of our redemption, how can it become a barrier to its completion?

That being the case, "If God is for us, who is against us? He who did not spare His own Son, but delivered Him over for us all, how will He not also with Him freely give us all things? Who will bring a charge against God's elect? God is the one who justifies; who is the one who condemns? Christ Jesus is He who died, yes, rather who was raised, who is at the right hand of God, who also intercedes for us" (Rom. 8:31-34). Although His work of atonement is finished, Christ's continuing ministry of intercession for those saved through His sacrifice will continue without interruption until every redeemed soul is safe in heaven. Just as Isaiah had prophesied, "He poured out Himself to death, and was numbered with the transgressors; yet He Himself bore the sin of many, and interceded for the transgressors" (Isa. 53:12). He "is able also to save forever those who draw near to God through Him, since He always lives to make intercession for them" (Heb. 7:25). Jesus pledged that He would lose none of God's elect, but bring them all to glory (see John 6:37-40).

The securing of our salvation is the function of Jesus' perpetual intercession for us. We can no more keep ourselves saved than we can save ourselves in the first place. But just as Jesus had the power to save us, He has the power to keep us. Constantly, eternally, perpetually Jesus Christ intercedes for us before His Father. Through Christ we are able to "stand in the presence of His glory blameless with great joy" (Jude 24). In His Son we are now blameless in the Father's sight. When we are glorified, we will be blameless in His presence. Don't let Satan get away with His accusations—you are secure in Christ. If we understand what Christ did on the cross to save us from sin, we understand what it means to be secure in His salvation. Through our remaining days on earth and throughout all eternity, our gracious Lord will hold us safe in His everlasting love by His everlasting power.

Pastor Peter Lewis offers a fitting summary of Christ's interceding on behalf of His own:

> Jesus Christ in his mediation does not operate as a third party, *moving between* God and believers, as though God would always be unapproachable; rather, he operates as *one* with God and his people, in whom believers are brought face to face with a Father who loves them, who delights to receive them, and who rejoices to make their persons and their prayers, their worship and their lives accepted in the beloved Son.
>
> I once heard of a picture which perfectly illustrates this. It was a large, typically Victorian religious piece of work, but the artist showed a striking degree of spiritual insight as well as originality in his composition. The scene was a storm on the lake of first-century Galilee. The foreground was dominated by a representation of Jesus' terrified disciples, rowing furiously through huge waves which threatened to engulf and overturn them at any moment. There seemed at first to be nothing else—no relief in the scene of fear and extreme danger. Then one's eye was taken by a shaft of sunlight through the storm-clouds to a rocky hillside on the shore. And there one saw, kneeling among the rocks, a praying figure. Many artists had painted the

later scene, Christ walking on the water "in the fourth watch of the night" (Matt. 14:22-3), but this artist had captured a reality just as profound when he depicted an earlier stage in the drama: Christ praying in the hills (v. 23) while His followers were battling the storm (v. 24)! It is the story of the Church militant as she works and wars for the Church triumphant. She is never alone (Matt. 28:20).[2]

With that picture in mind, why do so many believers, when faced with trials and temptation, go anywhere but to God's throne? Christ is there, ever ready to strengthen you, comfort you, and restore you. He is prepared to receive the sin-stained heart that you bring to Him and to clean it. And He is ever ready to dry your tears. All the resources are in Him. But you need to pursue Him to take advantage of those resources. To begin to do that, you need to return to your first love.

Notes

1. D. Martyn Lloyd-Jones, *Romans: The Final Perseverance of the Saints* (Grand Rapids, MI: Zondervan, 1975), p. 437.
2. Peter Lewis, *The Glory of Christ* (London: Hodder & Stoughton, 1992), pp. 387-388. Emphasis in original.

PART FOUR

JESUS OUR FIRST LOVE

LOVE AND OBEDIENCE

A famous lyric from an old, popular song says, "Love and marriage go together like a horse and carriage." When it comes to the spiritual realm, love and obedience also go together—one pulls the other. In this relationship, however, love is the driving force behind obedience because the biblical concept of love has nothing to do with emotion or sentimentality; it has everything to do with an act of the will. Jesus said it best: "If you love Me, you will keep My commandments" and "He who has My commandments and keeps them, is the one who loves Me" (John 14:15,21). Obedience to Christ and His Word is the ultimate proof of the reality of your love to Christ.

The Old Testament saints understood that kind of commitment. Deuteronomy 6:5 says, "You shall love the Lord your God with all your heart and with all your soul and with all your might." Their devotion to God was an all-consuming and wholehearted priority. Loving and obeying God were not optional. Neither was worshiping and serving Him.

Jesus affirmed that priority when a conniving lawyer asked Him which commandment in the Law was the greatest. Jesus said, " 'You shall love the Lord your God with all your heart, and with all your soul, and with all your mind.' This is the great and foremost commandment" (Matt. 22:37-38). That command is no less important for us. A consuming love for the Lord Jesus Christ ought to be the priority of our lives. In his first epistle, Peter sums up our priority when, speaking of Christ, he says, "Though you have not seen Him, you love Him" (1:8). Paul says that we ought to "love our Lord

Jesus Christ with incorruptible love" (Eph. 6:24). Love for Christ even takes precedence over our closest human relationships: "He who loves father or mother more than Me is not worthy of Me; and he who loves son or daughter more than Me is not worthy of Me" (Matt. 10:37). Ultimately, lack of love to Christ calls into question the genuineness of one's salvation: "If anyone does not love the Lord, he is to be accursed" (1 Cor. 16:22).

Puritan Thomas Vincent describes the ways in which our obedience reveals the reality of our love to Christ:

> Your love to Christ is known by your obedience unto Christ. If Christ is your beloved, He is also your Lord; if you have true affection for Him, you will yield subjection unto Him. If you love Christ, you are careful to please Christ; you are not the servants of the flesh, to take care to please the flesh, but you are the servants of Christ to take care, above all persons and all things, to please Christ. If you love Christ, you are fearful of giving just occasion of offense unto men but, above all, you are fearful of displeasing and offending your Lord. Do you labor so to walk that you may please Christ in the way of sincere and universal obedience? Are you hearty in your obedience unto Christ? Have you a respect to all His commandments? Is it your grief that you fall short in your obedience unto Christ? If you can say in the presence of the Lord and your hearts (do not give your tongues the lie) that you do not live and allow yourselves in the practice of any known sin which Christ forbids, nor in the neglect of any known duty which Christ commands, this is sure evidence of true love to Jesus Christ.[1]

When I look at Christ's church, I rarely see that kind of devotion, that kind of commitment, that sheer abandonment to the divine priorities. In many ways we give equal, if not greater, affection and devotion to the passing things of this world.

We live in a day when the vast majority of people in our world lack convictions about what their priorities ought to be because they are constantly bombarded by a myriad of options. Each day we make choices about what to eat, what to wear, and how to entertain ourselves. In the process we've allowed our faith and love for Christ to be reduced to a single choice among the many on our list of options. To many, what was once the priority on Sunday morning—going to church—is now just one of several choices. After all, since Sunday is a day off from work or school for most people, why not just play golf, take a drive, go to brunch, take in a ball game or a movie, go on a picnic, or just simply spend the day around the house and tinker or watch television.

In the midst of all the alternatives, Christians have allowed to slip the reality that their faith is ultimately made up of specific non-optionals. Instead of loving Him with all their being, many believers have learned to love the Lord Jesus Christ selectively. They may verbalize their love for Him, but the real question is whether or not it makes a difference in the way they live. They are willing to love the Lord if the price isn't too high, if it makes them feel comfortable, or if that's the best option at the time. Thomas Vincent describes what that lack of love to Christ communicates:

> It is observed, and it is greatly to be lamented, that there is, of late years, a great decay in the power of godliness among those that are sincere; and is it not evident in the great decay of love, even in true Christians, unto Jesus Christ? . . . Is it not evident that you have but little love to Christ when He is but little in your thoughts and meditations? . . . You can think often of your food, but how little do your thoughts feed upon Christ, who is the Bread of Life? You can often think of your raiment, but how little do you think of the robes of Christ's righteousness? You can think often of your earthly friends, but how little do you think of Jesus Christ, your friend in heaven? . . .
>
> Moreover, does it not argue little love to Christ that you speak so little *of* Him and *for* Him in your conversing one with another? If you had much love to Christ, would not this love breathe forth more in your discourses? . . .

You can readily discourse of news and public occurrences . . . but when you leave Christ quite out of your discourse, it shows that you have not an abundance of love to Him because, out of the abundance of the heart, the mouth will speak of their riches. Such as have much love to pleasures will be often speaking of that subject; such as love their friends much will be often speaking and commending them when they are in company. And when you speak but little of Christ, it is a sign that you love Him but little.[2]

Amazingly, Vincent wrote that in the seventeenth century, over 300 years ago, when people did not have the number of alternatives we have today. The problem for most Christians is not that they have altogether stopped loving Christ, for that would betray an unredeemed life, but that they have been diverted from their first love by the world's priorities.

We need to return to our first love. To do that (as I mentioned at the beginning of this book), we need to follow the three steps outlined by the Lord in Revelation 2:5: remember, repent and repeat. In the previous chapters, I've endeavored to help you remember by recalling for you who Christ is, what He has done, and what He is now doing for you. In this chapter and the next, we'll deal with our Lord's last two commands—repent and repeat. In this chapter, we'll focus on the necessity of repenting from our failure to love and obey Christ by seeing how our Lord dealt with one who failed Him miserably, yet was restored because of his repentant heart: the apostle Peter.

Peter's Failure

In all the history of redemption, few saints have fallen to the depths of sin and unfaithfulness that Peter did when he denied Jesus the night our Lord was arrested and put on trial for His life. Yet few saints have been so powerfully used by God as Peter was after he repented and was restored. The Gospel accounts of these two events in Peter's life give us great hope and encouragement that in spite of the severity of our sin against our Lord, He is always waiting to forgive and to restore. Nothing is more devastating to a believer than to realize he has denied the Lord by what he has said or not said, done or not done. Yet nothing is more exhilarating than knowing God's gracious forgiveness of unfaithfulness after it is confessed and the joy of greater usefulness.

His Descent

Peter's denial did not happen spontaneously in response to unexpected danger or embarrassment; he laid the groundwork that fateful night through a series of steps that eventually led to his collapse.

Peter's first step was his boast that "even though all may fall away because of You, I will never fall away" (Matt. 26:33). That revealed his unfounded self-confidence and directly contradicted His Lord's prediction that *all* the disciples would fall away that very night (see v. 31).

His second step toward his collapse was his blatant denial of Christ's specific prediction: "Truly I say to you that this very night, before a cock crows, you will deny Me three times.' Peter said to Him, 'Even if I have to die with You, I will not deny You'" (vv. 34-35).

Peter's next fateful step was his prayerlessness. Jesus took Peter, James and John with Him to keep watch for Him while He spoke intimately with the Father. But instead of being alert to the coming hour of darkness, they simply went to sleep. When Jesus returned and found them so, He said, "So, you men could not keep watch with Me for one hour? Keep watching and praying that you may not enter into temptation" (vv. 40-41). But they did not take seriously His warnings and were indifferent to His call for prayer.

The next step in Peter's collapse was his impulsiveness.

When the crowd came to arrest Jesus, Peter tried to decapitate Malchus, the servant of the high priest, but missed and cut off his ear (see v. 51). Peter refused to believe that God's plan was for Christ to suffer and die.

The final step leading to Peter's denial of Christ was his compromise in allowing himself to flee away from His Lord and then linger in a place of danger—the courtyard of the high priest (see v. 58)—where his loyalty would be tested beyond his courage. He had boasted too much, spoken too soon, prayed too little, acted too fast, and wandered too far.

His Collapse

Once he arrived in the courtyard, Peter "sat down with the officers to see the outcome" (v. 58) of the trial. He should have known what the outcome would be; the Lord had told him enough times previously. As he kept vigil, he hoped to go unnoticed in the crowd of people assembled in the large courtyard.

Sometime after 1 A.M., about the time the trial began, "Peter was sitting outside in the courtyard, and a servant-girl came to him and said, 'You too were with Jesus the Galilean'" (v. 69). Apparently Peter spoke first to the girl, "Woman, I do not know Him" (Luke 22:57), and then "he denied it before them all, saying, 'I do not know what you are talking about'" (Matt. 26:70). A few hours earlier Peter had vowed to die before he would forsake Christ, yet he denied even knowing Him.

To escape embarrassment, Peter inconspicuously "went out onto the porch" (Mark 14:68), which evidently was near the gateway. But in spite of his precautions, "a little later" (Luke 22:58), "another servant-girl saw him and said to those who were there, 'This man was with Jesus of Nazareth'" (Matt. 26:71). An unidentified man also joined in the accusation, saying, "You are one of them too!" (Luke 22:58). To the girl, Peter "denied . . . with an oath, 'I do not know the man'" (Matt. 26:72), and to the man he said, "Man, I am not!" (Luke 22:58). This time he added an oath to his lie, hoping to reinforce his deceit about an hour later (see v. 59): "the bystanders came up and said to Peter, 'Surely you too are one of them; for even the way you talk gives you away'" (Matt. 26:73). Peter could not hide his Galilean accent. Still refusing either to claim or to rely on Jesus, "he began to curse and swear, 'I do not know the man!'" (v. 74). The Greek word translated "to curse" is a strong term that involved pronouncing death on oneself at the hand of God if one were lying. As the accusations became more specific and incriminating, Peter's denials became more intense and extreme.

Then the worst imaginable moment happened: "Immediately, while he was still speaking, a rooster crowed. The Lord turned and looked at Peter" (Luke 22:60-61). Peter must have been able to see the Lord. He may have been standing outside looking in on the trial when the cock crowed. It's also possible that the trial had ended and as Jesus was being led away, He passed by at the moment Peter denied Him for the third time. No matter how it happened, the eyes of the Lord must have penetrated Peter's soul, burning deep into his heart and conscience the evil of his sin.

As if that visual indictment weren't enough, while he stood transfixed by his Lord's eyes, his conscience assaulted him as he "remembered the word of the Lord, how He had told him, 'Before a rooster crows today, you will deny Me three times'" (v. 61). Peter's already unbearable anguish was made even more unbearable.

Peter's Repentance

Fortunately Peter's true character is not revealed in his denial, but in his repentance, which began with deep remorse. Overwhelmed by His Savior's love and grace and by his own sin and unfaithfulness, Peter "went out and wept bitterly" (v. 62). It was not until Peter saw the Lord's face and remembered His words that he came to his senses, acknowledged his sin, and repented of his failure. He surrendered his sin to Christ for forgiveness and cleansing.

Peter's Restoration

In spite of his repentance, Peter still had much to learn about what Jesus required of him. He had sinned by what he did in those denials, and he would sin again by what he did not do. After our Lord was resurrected, He told the women who saw Him first to tell His disciples "to leave for Galilee, and there they will see Me"

(Matt. 28:10). The Lord appeared to His disciples on two separate occasions before they "proceeded to Galilee, to the mountain which Jesus had designated" (Matt. 28:16). John 21:2 tells us that there were together "Simon Peter, and Thomas called Didymus, and Nathanael of Cana in Galilee, and the sons of Zebedee [James and John], and two others of His disciples [probably Philip and Andrew]." They were obedient to a point—they initially went to Galilee and to the mountain the Lord designated. But as time passed and Jesus didn't appear right away, Peter's impulsiveness took over.

The Failure to Love
"Simon Peter said to them, 'I am going fishing.' They said to him, 'We will also come with you'" (v. 3). Peter was the leader, and he led the rest of the disciples into outright disobedience of the Lord. He was given a simple command, and he disobeyed it; he failed to do what he was told. It's possible Peter thought he was of little use to the Lord, especially since he disappointed Him when it really counted. So he decided to return to the line of work he knew best, and the other disciples, perhaps sensing their own failures as well, returned with him. Ultimately it doesn't matter what their reasoning was or what their feelings were toward Jesus, their love for Him failed as evidenced by their disobedience. Peter and the other disciples found out quickly the consequences of that disobedience: "They went out and got into the boat; and that night they caught nothing" (v. 3). Peter's self-reliance was useless when it came up against the Lord's will for him. Since he couldn't make it as a disciple, he decided he could still rely on his own ability to catch fish. But he quickly discovered that that aspect of his life was over.

The Restoration of Love
The Lord now begins the process of restoring Peter:

> When the day was now breaking, Jesus stood on the beach; yet the disciples did not know that it was Jesus. So Jesus

said to them, "Children, you do not have any fish, do you?" They answered Him, "No." And He said to them, "Cast the net on the right-hand side of the boat and you will find a catch." So they cast, and then they were not able to haul it in because of the great number of fish. Therefore that disciple [John] whom Jesus loved said to Peter, "It is the Lord" (vv. 4-7).

John may have been recalling the earlier time when Jesus called these same men to follow Him. On that occasion the Lord performed a similar rerouting of the fish in the Sea of Galilee. After teaching the people from Peter's boat, Jesus commanded Peter:

"Put out into the deep water and let down your nets for a catch." Simon answered and said, "Master, we worked hard all night and caught nothing, but I will do as You say and let down the nets." When they had done this, they enclosed a great quantity of fish, and their nets began to break; so they signaled to their partners in the other boat for them to come and help them. And they came and filled both of the boats, so that they began to sink. But when Simon Peter saw that, he fell down at Jesus' feet, saying, "Go away from me Lord, for I am a sinful man!" For amazement had seized him and all his companions because of the catch of fish which they had taken; and so also were James and John, sons of Zebedee, who were partners with Simon. And Jesus said to Simon, "Do not fear, from now on you will be catching men." And when they had brought their boats to land, they left everything and followed Him (Luke 5:4-11).

That may have been the last time they had been in that boat, and now, more than three years later, the Lord had to repeat the same lesson. He didn't call them to follow Him so that after He was gone they could return to their old life; He called them so that they might carry on His work of making disciples of all nations (see Matt. 28:19). But to do that, He had to reestablish their priorities:

> When Simon Peter heard that it was the Lord, he put his outer garment on (for he was stripped for work), and threw himself into the sea. But the other disciples came in the little boat, for they were not far from the land, but about one hundred yards away, dragging the net full of fish. So when they got out on the land, they saw a charcoal fire already laid and fish placed on it, and bread. Jesus said to them, "Bring some of the fish which you have now caught." Simon Peter went up and drew the net to land, full of large fish, a hundred and fifty-three, and although there were so many, the net was not torn. Jesus said to them, "Come and have breakfast." None of the disciples ventured to question Him, "Who are You?" knowing that it was the Lord. Jesus came and took the bread and gave it to them, and the fish likewise. This is now the third time that Jesus was manifested to the disciples, after He was raised from the dead (John 21:7-14).

Notice that the Lord, the one who had been offended by Peter and the other disciples, initiated their restoration. Many Christians, having failed to love the Lord as they ought, drift away from Him in shame over their sin. But all believers need to realize that their Savior is eager for them to return to Him and be restored to fellowship. In Jeremiah 31:3 the Lord says, "I have loved you with an everlasting love." Nothing can separate us from the love of Christ, not even our own disobedience or our failure to love Him as we should. We can be thankful for His love which is unending and will reach out to recover us.

Those who become complacent about their failure, however, and don't desire to restore their relationship to Christ, become comfortable with a superficial brand of Christianity that avoids the priorities of God's kingdom. If that becomes true of you, joy and peace are gone and God won't bless you, but He may bring you under His chastening hand. Peter wanted restoration.

The Requirement of Love

After serving breakfast to the disciples, Jesus said to Simon Peter, "Simon, son of John, do you love Me more than these?" (John 21:15). The Greek word translated "love" is the familiar *agapao,* which is the highest kind of love, the noblest kind of devotion. It is the love of the will, not the emotions or feelings. It chooses to love.

By asking Peter if he supremely loved Him more than "these," Jesus may have been referring to the other disciples or to the trappings of his former life—his boat, his nets, and life on the sea as a fisherman. Jesus confronted Peter about his priorities: Did he love Christ more than his own life—more than his own plans, desires and pleasures?

Peter's response was a carefully measured one: "Yes, Lord; You know that I love You" (v. 15). We see a different word for "love" in Peter's response: *phileo,* which refers to tender affection. It seems Peter couldn't claim *agapao,* the supreme love for Christ; that would have been blatant hypocrisy when measured against his behavior. The Lord then told him, "Tend My lambs" (v. 15). That command was a direct reminder to Peter that he was no longer a fisherman; he was now a shepherd of God's sheep.

Our Lord wasn't finished with Peter: "He said to him again a second time, 'Simon, son of John, do you love Me?' He said to Him, 'Yes, Lord; You know that I love You.' He said to him, 'Shepherd My sheep.' He said to him the third time, 'Simon, son of John, do you love Me?'" (vv. 16-17). On this third occasion, Jesus used the word for "love" that Peter had used—*phileo.* Thus Jesus was even questioning Peter's affection for Him. "Peter was grieved because He said to him the third time, 'Do you love Me?' And he said to Him, 'Lord, You know all things; You know that I love You.' Jesus said to him, 'Tend My sheep'" (v. 17). Peter was deeply hurt that his Lord doubted his *phileo* love.

It seems apparent that to coincide with Peter's three denials, three times Jesus questioned the validity of Peter's love for Him. As was true for Peter, the depth of your love for Christ must be demonstrated by your obedience. The test of love is not emotion or sentiment; the ultimate proof is in your obedience to Him.

The Cost of Love

Having established love as the most important ingredient in restoring their relationship, Christ delineates a closely related component: " 'Truly, truly, I say to you, when you were younger, you used to gird yourself and walk wherever you wished; but when you grow old, you will stretch out your hands [be put to death on a cross] and someone else will gird you, and bring you where you do not wish to go.' Now this He said, signifying by what kind of death he would glorify God" (vv. 18-19).

There is always a cost attached to loving Christ, and that is a willingness to sacrifice for Him. Here Jesus was prophesying the martyrdom Peter would face. But He was also informing him that a necessary aspect of their relationship was Peter's willingness to give his life for Christ.

Jesus Himself identified sacrifice as the supreme mark of love: "Greater love has no one than this, that one lay down his life for his friends" (15:13). Whatever you are willing to sacrifice in your life for Christ is evidence of the depth of your love. Whatever you are unwilling to sacrifice will expose the shallowness of your love.

Jesus' last command for Peter was, "Follow Me" (21:19,22). Our Lord's restoration of Peter was now complete, and it ended with a command—one that Peter would obey. The time came when the apostle would not deny his Lord or disobey Him—and he was executed for it. Tradition says he was crucified upside down.

Obedience to the Lord is what demonstrates genuine love for Him. When He is the priority of our lives, we will be willing to obey Him and thus prove our love to Him. But it doesn't come easily. Thomas Vincent appropriately says:

Let your love show itself in the willingness of your obedience. Serve the Lord with a willing and ready mind, with alacrity and cheerfulness of spirit, looking upon the service of Christ as your honor, and esteeming every duty as your privilege. If you have any constraints upon obedience, let them be constraints of love, as 2 Corinthians 5:14. If you are forced to obey Christ, let there be no violence but the violence of love; if you are dragged to duty, let it be with no other cords than the cords of love. Let love be the spur and goad to prick you forward that you may not only walk but run in the ways of Christ's commandments with an enlarged heart.[3]

If you are ever going to have a meaningful relationship with your Lord and Savior—if you are ever going to return to your first love—you must begin by obeying Him. There are no shortcuts. In the next chapter, we'll look at some of the ways Scripture encourages and motivates believers to do just that.

Notes
1. Thomas Vincent, *The True Christian's Love to the Unseen Christ* (Ligonier, PA: Soli Deo Gloria, 1993), pp. 24-25.
2. Ibid., pp. 30-31. Emphasis in original.
3. Ibid., p. 87.

IN PURSUIT OF OUR FIRST LOVE

When I was in college, I had the privilege of being a member of the school's track and field team. I performed best in the sprints, and occasionally the quarter mile. One of my favorite races was the mile relay. Of all the races we ran, the one I remember best is one we didn't win.

The race started wonderfully—our first runner ran such a great opening quarter-mile leg that as he passed the baton to me, we were tied for the lead. I ran as hard as I could, hoping to at least maintain our position if not put us in front. As I passed the baton to our third runner, we were in first place. I thought we had an excellent chance to win—our fourth runner was especially fast.

Our third runner took off around the first curve and down the back stretch, holding on to our lead. And then the unthinkable happened. He stopped suddenly, walked off the track, and sat down on the grass. I ran over to him, thinking that he must have pulled a muscle. When I reached him, he didn't look like he was in pain, so I asked what was wrong. I'll never forget his reply. All he said was, "I don't know—I just didn't feel like running."

Sadly, many Christians are like that runner. Somewhere along the way they stopped pursuing a deep, loving relationship with Christ, walked off His path of righteousness, and sat down to rest in their own self-righteousness and the ease of worldly pleasures. In so doing they left their first love, just as the church at Ephesus did. The only way to get back in the race is to "remember from where you have fallen, and repent and do the deeds you did at first" (Rev. 2:5).

That's what we have been endeavoring to do throughout this book. We have focused the major portion of it on what our beloved

Savior and Lord has done and is doing for us. In the previous chapter we looked at the apostle Peter's denial of Christ and his subsequent repentance and restoration to love, ending with our Lord's command to "Follow Me." It is to that command we turn our attention in this chapter. To "do the deeds you did at first," you must understand that your allegiance and love to Christ demands a lifelong commitment. As our Lord Himself said, "No one, after putting his hand to the plow and looking back, is fit for the kingdom of God" (Luke 9:62).

The apostle Paul understood well that priority. His relationship to Christ was the passion of his life: "that I may know Him and the power of His resurrection and the fellowship of His sufferings, being conformed to His death; in order that I may attain to the resurrection from the dead" (Phil. 3:10-11). But he was under no illusion that he had achieved anything, comparing his own pursuit of Christ to that of a runner in a race:

> Not that I have already obtained it or have already become perfect, but I press on so that I may lay hold of that for which also I was laid hold of by Christ Jesus. Brethren, I do not regard myself as having laid hold of it yet; but one thing I do: forgetting what lies behind and reaching forward to what lies ahead, I press on toward the goal for the prize of the upward call of God in Christ Jesus. Let us therefore, as many as are perfect, have this attitude; and if in anything you have a different attitude, God will reveal that also to you; however, let us keep living by that same standard to which we have attained (vv. 12-16).

Running the Race

To Paul, the Christian life was a permanent pursuit of Christ—every day entering into a deeper and richer relationship with Him. He did not rest on all that he had been given in Christ (see Phil. 3:7-11). On the contrary, he had a humble, honest assessment of his own imperfection: "Not that I have already obtained it, or have already become perfect" (v. 12). We are not yet what we should be, what we can be, or what we will be when we see the Lord. Our spiritual race begins with a sense of dissatisfaction—there's no reason to even begin the race without it. F.B. Meyer wisely observed that "self-dissatisfaction lies at the root of our noblest achievements."[1]

If a man like Paul, who knew Christ in the most intimate way, didn't rest but kept pursuing a greater knowledge of his Lord, how much more should we endeavor to grow in our relationship to Christ? If you are to renew your first love, you must begin your pursuit of Christ the same way Paul did—with the awareness that you have much learning and growing to do. Once you start, there are several principles you need to apply as you pursue Him.

Maximum Effort

Considering who Christ is and what He has done for us, our effort should not be less than Paul's: "I press on so that I may lay hold of that for which also I was laid hold of by Christ Jesus" (v. 12). The Greek word translated "press on" (*dioko*) was used of a sprinter who ran aggressively. That was the kind of effort Paul exerted—he ran to Christ with all his might, straining every spiritual muscle to win the prize (see 1 Cor. 9:24-27). That ought to be our mindset as well. The writer of Hebrews encouraged us to "lay aside every encumbrance and the sin which so easily entangles us, and let us run with endurance the race that is set before us" (12:1). As a Christian, there's only one race you ought to be running—and this one takes maximum effort using the means of grace God has provided for us.

No one is going to put forth that kind of effort, however, unless there is some reward at the end. For Paul, and us as well, it is "that for which also I was laid hold of by Christ Jesus" (Phil. 3:12). Paul's prize, and ours, is the very purpose God had in saving us: "Whom He foreknew, He also predestined to become conformed to the image of His Son" (Rom. 8:29). God saved us so that we might become like Christ, and as a result, that should be our lifelong pursuit. Paul also said, "It was for this He called you through our gospel, that you may gain the glory of our Lord Jesus Christ" (2 Thess. 2:14; see also Eph. 1:4).

Becoming like Christ is our most worthy goal in this life; that's why it requires a lifelong commitment and effort. Paul pursued becoming like the One he so deeply loved.

Focused Concentration

If an athlete competing in a race stands any chance of winning, he must focus on the finish and avoid the distractions along the track, the other competitors, and even the crowd. Likewise, the Christian must concentrate on attaining the goal of Christlikeness and not get distracted by worldly attractions and temptations. Paul was well aware of those dangers. That's why he said, "I do not regard myself as having laid hold of it [Christlikeness] yet; but one thing I do: forgetting what lies behind and reaching forward to what lies ahead" (Phil. 3:13). Paul was consumed with only one purpose in his life: "the prize of the upward call of God in Christ Jesus" (v. 14). That prize is being made like Christ (see 1 John 3:2). That is the believer's eternal reward and should be our temporal pursuit. We will, when called up to heaven, be like Christ. That prize is our present goal as well.

I wish more believers had the same desire to focus on Christlikeness. Unfortunately, too many follow the lead of the "double-minded man, [who is] unstable in all his ways" (Jas. 1:8). They have a divided allegiance. Regaining your first love and focusing on Christ calls for two attitudes.

Forget the Past

As a runner approaches the starting line, his past performances have no bearing on the race he is preparing to run. The same thing is true when we run the spiritual race in pursuit of Christ—the past is completely irrelevant. Your successes and failures in the past are insignificant to the present, let alone the future. You can't evaluate your usefulness by your former virtuous deeds and achievements in ministry; neither should you be debilitated by past sins and failures. Unfortunately, too many Christians are distracted by the past and, as a result, don't make current progress in the race.

Reach for the Goal

Instead of looking back, a good runner is always "reaching forward to what lies ahead" (Phil. 3:13). The Greek word for "reaching forward" is *epekteino*, and it refers to an intense stretching to the limit of one's capacity. Commentator William Hendricksen writes, "The verb in the original is very graphic. It pictures the runner straining every nerve and muscle as he keeps on running with all his might toward the goal, his hand stretched out as if to grasp it."[2] To run like that, you must forget the past and concentrate only on the goal ahead. Do you have that kind of concentration in your desire to become like Christ? To effectively pursue Christ, we must focus all our concentration on becoming like Him.

Spiritual Motivation

Paul was highly motivated in his pursuit of Christ: "I press on toward the goal for the prize of the upward call of God in Christ Jesus" (v. 14). He was motivated by spiritual matters; he was not caught up in material comforts and worldly pursuits. His goal was to be like Christ, and he would receive his reward when God's upward call came. Christlikeness is both the goal and the prize that we pursue.

At the end of his life Paul could say with great confidence, "I have fought the good fight, I have finished the course, I have kept the faith; in the future there is laid up for me the crown of righteousness, which the Lord, the righteous Judge, will award to me on that day; and not only to me, but also to all who have loved His appearing" (2 Tim. 4:7-8). Paul fought the battles, ran the race, and guarded the faith because of his love for Christ. He did so because he longed for the day when he would be like Him completely—the day when He would appear (see 1 John 3:2).

The goal of your life as a Christian is to love Christ and, in loving Him, to become like Him. That's what happens when you have an intimate relationship with someone. After many years together, for example, husbands and wives begin to take on each other's character qualities. In a similar yet even more profound way, the same thing happens as you pursue Christ. The more you look to

Him, the more His characteristics become your characteristics.

Preoccupation with the world and material possessions serves no worthwhile purpose for the Christian. Such a pursuit will only divert you from your proper motivation, which is to be like Christ. The apostle John said, "The one who says he abides in [Christ] ought himself to walk in the same manner as He walked" (1 John 2:6). If you claim that Christ means everything to you, then you ought to pursue Him with every ounce of your energy.

Such a pursuit is objective, not subjective. It is not a mystical experience, but an exposure to the truth about Christ revealed in the Bible. The knowledge of Christ is gained and enriched only in the Scripture that speaks of Him. The Bible is the mirror in which His glory is reflected. When we gaze at it intently, we become like Him. Paul said, "We all, with unveiled face, beholding as in a mirror the glory of the Lord, are being transformed into the same image from glory to glory, just as from the Lord, the Spirit" (2 Cor. 3:18).

Divine Assistance

Most Christians do not pursue Christ with the intensity of the apostle Paul. And some have actually stopped running. Those people may be either preoccupied with the past or content with their present condition. Instead of recognizing their need, they justify the level they have attained.

Every believer ought to have the attitude that he or she is not perfect (see Phil. 3:15). Those who have that perspective regarding their spirituality will be ready to respond positively to God's correction. However, many believers do not have that attitude. But rest assured, if you have the wrong attitude about your spirituality, if you're content with the current level of your spiritual growth, then God will reveal your true condition.

Sometimes the Lord will bring chastening into our lives when we have lost the right perspective (see Heb. 12:5-11). At other times, He will bring trials into our lives to reveal our true condition and to build and strengthen our faith and trust in Him (see Jas. 1:2,4).

Consistent Effort

No one can win a race with intermittent effort. Christlikeness cannot be reached with that kind of effort either—it is an ongoing pursuit. So Paul says, "Let us keep living by that same standard to which we have attained" (Phil. 3:16). The Greek verb translated "keep living" refers to walking in line. Just as a runner must stay in his lane and keep up the same effort until he reaches the finish, Christians must stay in line spiritually and keep moving forward toward the goal of Christlikeness.

One summer I had the opportunity to visit Europe and in particular the Alps. At the foot of one of those majestic mountains is a famous gravestone. Underneath the individual's name the epitaph reads, "He died climbing." That ought to be our attitude as we pursue Christ. When the time comes for us to go to be with the Lord, we ought to be in the process of pursuing Him when He calls us home.

Focusing on the Finish

Home is the Christian's focus because that is the end of the race. To encourage the Philippian believers in their pursuit of Christ, Paul said, "Our citizenship is in heaven, from which also we eagerly wait for a Savior, the Lord Jesus Christ" (3:20). As we look to the finish line, two great realities must occupy our minds: we focus on our Lord who is in heaven, and we anticipate His coming to take us there.

Our Heavenly Goal

In our pursuit of Christ, our track, as it were, is upward. It may begin on earth, but it ends in heaven, "where Christ is, seated at the right hand of God" (Col. 3:1). As we run in pursuit of Him, we are no longer being "conformed to this world," but we are being "transformed by the renewing of [our minds]" (Rom. 12:2).

Preoccupation with heavenly reality is the hallmark of true spirituality. It is only when we rise above the world that we learn to fix our minds on heavenly realities. Our blessings are in heaven (see Eph. 1:3); Christ is there (see v. 20); and we, through our union with Him in His resurrection, exist in the heavenly realm (see 2:6). Because we "have been raised up with Christ" (Col. 3:1), we are alive to the realities of the divine realm. When we were saved, the world ceased to be our home. We now have "our citizenship . . . in heaven" (Phil. 3:20).

The Greek word translated "citizenship" is used only in this verse and refers to a colony of foreigners. That certainly is true of Christians. We are the citizens of a foreign place to this world—heaven.

In Colossians 3:1 Paul said that we are to "keep seeking the things above." Preoccupation with the eternal realities that are ours in Christ is to be the pattern of the believer's life. Jesus put it this way: "Seek first His kingdom and His righteousness, and all these things will be added to you" (Matt. 6:33).

Our preoccupation with heaven will govern our earthly responses. When we are preoccupied with the One who reigns there, we will view the things, people and events of this world through His eyes and with an eternal perspective. As we keep our focus on the heavenlies, we will live out our heavenly values in this world to the glory of God.

The thoughts of heaven that ought to fill our minds must derive from Scripture. The Bible is the only reliable source of knowledge about the character of God and the values of heaven. In it we learn about the things that should occupy our thoughts (see Phil. 4:8). As such heavenly values dominate our minds, they will produce godly behavior and make us more like the Christ we love (see 2 Cor. 3:18). As we continue to fix "our eyes on Jesus the author and perfecter of faith" (Heb. 12:2), we will become more like Him.

Our Returning Savior

The more we love Him, the more we love His appearing (see 2 Tim. 4:8). We look forward to the day when Christ comes to take us home. "We eagerly wait for a Savior, the Lord Jesus Christ" (Phil. 3:20). When Christ returns for us, the race is over. That's why we look forward to that day as we continue to pursue Him. Thus the anticipation of our Lord's return is a great source of spiritual motivation, accountability and security.

Knowing that Jesus is coming provides tremendous motivation in reaching for the prize, because we'll want to be ready when He comes. We find motivation in the hope of one day being rewarded by Christ and hearing, "Well done, good and faithful slave . . . enter into the joy of your master" (Matt. 25:23).

Christ's return also provides us with accountability. We know that "each one of us will give account of himself to God" (Rom. 14:12) and that "if any man's work is burned up, he will suffer loss" (1 Cor. 3:15). That accountability alone ought to keep us pursuing Christ.

We can also rest secure in the fact of Christ's imminent return. In John 6:39 Jesus says, "This is the will of Him who sent Me, that of all that He has given Me I lose nothing, but raise it up on the last day."

Christ's return is not just an event in God's plan; it is the fulfillment of our lifelong desire. We eagerly anticipate the day when finally we will be in the presence of the One who has been the object of our love.

Breaking the Tape

In a race, only one runner gets to break the tape at the finish line, and that person is the winner. But in the spiritual race of our pursuit of Christ, every believer gets to break the tape because every true Christian has already won. The day is almost at hand when we will cross the finish line into the heavenly realm and receive the prize, which consists of two glorious events: the transformation of our bodies and the bestowal of our divine inheritance.

Our Glorious Transformation

Paul says that when Christ returns, He "will transform the body of our humble state into conformity with the body of His glory" (Phil. 3:21). We look forward to His coming because we desire to be transformed. We long to be free from our sinful flesh and be perfect like Christ (see Rom. 8:23). While we have been made a new creation in the inner man, that inner man is incarcerated in unredeemed flesh. Our fallen humanness and its lusts remain with us. The new creation within us longs to be liberated from the sin that remains.

If we die any time before Christ comes for His own, our bodies go into the grave. Our spirits, however, immediately go to be with the Lord (see 2 Cor. 5:8; Phil. 1:23). Our bodies then await the second coming of Christ. At that time He will raise them all (see 1 Thess. 4:16) and transform them.

When God transforms our bodies, He will redesign and refashion them into ones adapted to an eternal, holy heaven. We will then be like Christ after His resurrection. Paul says we will be transformed "into conformity with the body of His glory" (Phil. 3:21). We know that "when He appears, we will be like Him, because we will see Him just as He is" (1 John 3:2). God not only has saved us from hell and given us heaven, but He also will make us like His Son.

When we die, our spirits are instantly perfected. When Christ returns, our bodies are raised and transformed to be like Christ as holy instruments for worship and service. We will never again have an evil impulse or an errant motive. Our minds and hearts will be filled with the pure light of God's truth and undiluted love, joy, peace and goodness. We ought to long for that with all our hearts.

Our Divine Inheritance

On the day we break the tape and enter fully into the Father's eternal heavenly kingdom, we will receive our promised inheritance (see Eph. 1:11). Our heavenly Father's resources are limitless, so our spiritual inheritance is limitless, because, as His fellow heirs, we share in everything that the Son of God, Jesus Christ, inherits. God has appointed Jesus Christ the "heir of all things" (Heb. 1:2), and because we are fellow heirs with Him (see Rom. 8:17), we will receive all that He receives!

On that day we will sit on the heavenly throne with Christ and rule there with Him (see Rev. 3:21), bearing forever the very image of our Savior and Lord (see 1 Cor. 15:49). In His great High

Priestly Prayer, Jesus spoke to His Father of the incredible and staggering truth that everyone who believes in Him will be one with Him and will share His full glory: "The glory which You have given Me I have given to them; that they may be one, just as We are one" (John 17:22). It is not that we will become gods, but that we will receive, by our joint inheritance with Christ, all the blessings and grandeur that God has.

One day everything on earth will perish and disappear, because the whole earth is defiled and corrupted. By great and marvelous contrast, however, one day every believer will "obtain an inheritance which is imperishable and undefiled and will not fade away" (1 Pet. 1:4). It is that very inheritance that is "reserved in heaven" for us. What a wonderful prize awaits us when we cross the finish line in pursuit of our glorious Lord and Savior.

Training for the Race

Just as athletes train to run in a race, all believers need to be in constant training because our race is lifelong. In his book *The True Christian's Love to the Unseen Christ*, Thomas Vincent offers nine principles that we should always be practicing in our pursuit of Christ.[3] They make a fitting climax to this study, because they encapsulate the very deeds that Christ would have us repeat (see Rev. 2:5):

Direction 1: "Be much in contemplation of Christ."[4] If you are to ever return to your first love, your first priority is to meditate on Christ. Don't let one day go by without taking the time to dwell on Him: on who He is, what He has done, and what He is doing for you. Vincent suggests, "Spend time in secret retirement, and there think and think again of the superlative excellencies and perfections which are in Christ's person; how wonderful and matchless His love is, what heights that cannot be reached, what depths in it that cannot be fathomed, what other dimensions which cannot be comprehended."[5]

Direction 2: "Be much in reading and studying the Scriptures."[6] The Bible is God's Word to you. It is where we find everything we need to know about our great Lord and Savior. Paul said that we are to "let the word of Christ richly dwell within [us]" (Col. 3:16). It is our spiritual food (see Matt. 4:4). To not feed on its truths every day is like going without food for a day. You wouldn't do that to your physical body, so why would you do that to your soul?

Direction 3: "Be much in prayer to God for this love."[7] Jesus said, "How much more will your Father who is in heaven give what is good to those who ask Him!" (Matt. 7:11). I can't think of anything better than having supreme love to Christ, and God will certainly give that to us if we ask Him for it sincerely. Vincent says, "If you would have much love to Christ in your hearts, you must be often at the throne of grace upon your knees, and there humbly acknowledge if not the lack, yet the weakness, of your love to Christ. Bewail your sins which dampen your affections, and earnestly request that He would work your hearts unto a strong love. Be importunate in prayer for this."[8]

Direction 4: "Get much faith."[9] This directive goes hand in hand with prayer. The writer of Hebrews said, "Faith is the assurance of things hoped for, the conviction of things not seen" (Heb. 11:1). Peter said of Christ, "Though you have not seen Him, you love Him" (1 Pet. 1:8). We can apprehend Christ in no other way but by faith, thus that is the only way we can truly love Him. Vincent says, "According to the measure of your faith, so will the measure of your love be. Such as are without any faith are without any love; such as have but feeble faith have but weak love; and such as have the strongest faith have the strongest love."[10]

Direction 5: "Labor for much of the Spirit; labor for much of the light of the Spirit."[11] The only way to truly love Christ is to "be filled with the Spirit" (Eph. 5:18). Jesus Himself gave the reason that the Holy Spirit has such a crucial role in our pursuit of Christ: "I will ask the Father, and He will give you another Helper, that He may be with you forever; that is the Spirit of truth, whom the world cannot receive, because it does not see Him or know Him, but you know Him because He abides with you and will be in you" (John 14:16-17).

Direction 6: "Labor for clear evidences of His love unto you." Vincent adds, "the apprehensions of Christ's loveliness may excite to some love, but the full, well-grounded persuasions of Christ's love to you will, above all, heighten your love to Christ."[12] If you are a true Christian, Christ loves you. But if you lack the assurance of your salvation, examine your life to make sure you are saved. Don't doubt our Lord's love, for Paul said, "God demonstrates His own love toward us, in that while we were yet sinners, Christ died for us" (Rom. 5:8).

Direction 7: "Get much hatred of sin and, accordingly, watch, pray, strive, and fight against sin as the worst of evils, as that which so much displeases your Lord."[13] When you do sin, go to the Lord and confess it so that you might experience the joy of restoration. Vincent encourages us further:

Disturb sin as much as you can; wage war every day with your remaining lusts. Let no day pass over your heads without giving some blows, some thrusts and wounds to sin. The more you straiten the room of sin in your hearts, the less room Christ will have there. Particularly, take heed of inordinate love to the world and the things in the world, the prevalence of which love will dampen your love to Christ. By how much more the world gets of your love, by so much the less Christ will have it.[14]

Direction 8: "Associate yourselves most with those that have most love unto Christ."[15] Simply stated, follow godly examples. Paul said, "Join in following my example, and observe those who walk according to the pattern you have in us" (Phil. 3:17).

Direction 9: "Be much in exercise of this love; hereby it is increased and heightened."[16] This last directive takes us back to the beginning. If we are to continually pursue Christ, we must be pursuing Him and practicing each of these directives every day. In every activity, in every contact, and in every thought, Christ is to be your focus. When you make Him your priority, you encourage the faithful and convict the unregenerate. When you love Christ with all your heart, soul and strength, God is glorified.

Some years ago I wrote a song about my desire to be like Christ. I hope it expresses the desire of your heart.

O to be like Thee, dear Jesus, my plea,
Just to know Thou art formed fully in me.
On with Thy beauty, Lord, off with my sin,
Fixed on Thy glory, Thy likeness to win.
O to be like Thee, Thine image display,
This is the Spirit's work day after day.
Glory to glory, transformed by His grace,
Till in Thy presence I stand face to face.
O to be like Thee, Thou lover of men,
Gracious and gentle, compassionate friend,
Merciful Savior, such kindness and care
Are only mine when Your likeness I share.

J.M.

Notes
1. F.B. Meyer, *The Epistle to the Philippians: A Devotional Commentary* (Grand Rapids, MI: Baker Books, 1952), p. 175.
2. William Hendricksen, *New Testament Commentary: Exposition of Philippians* (Grand Rapids, MI: Baker Books, 1979), p. 173.
3. Thomas Vincent, *The True Christian's Love to the Unseen Christ* (Ligonier, PA: Soli Deo Gloria, 1993), p. 75.
4. Ibid.
5. Ibid.
6. Ibid., p. 78.
7. Ibid., p. 79.
8. Ibid., p. 80.
9. Ibid., p. 81.
10. Ibid.
11. Ibid., p. 82.
12. Ibid.
13. Ibid., p. 83.
14. Ibid., p. 84.
15. Ibid.
16. Ibid., p. 85.

PERSONAL AND GROUP STUDY GUIDE

Before beginning your personal or group study of *A Simple Christianity,* take time to read these introductory comments.

If you are working through the study on your own, you may want to adapt certain sections (for example, the icebreakers), and record your responses to all questions in a separate notebook. You might find it more enriching or motivating to study with a partner with whom you can share answers or insights.

If you are leading a group, you may want to ask your group members to read each assigned chapter and work through the study questions before the group meets. This isn't always easy for busy adults, so encourage them with occasional phone calls or notes between meetings. Help members manage their time by suggesting that they identify a regular time of the day or week that they can devote to the study. They too may want to write their responses to the questions in a notebook. *To help keep group discussion focused on the material in* A Simple Christianity, *it is important that each member have his or her own copy of the book.*

Notice that each session includes the following features:

- **Chapter Theme:** a brief statement summarizing the chapter

- **Icebreaker:** an activity to help each member get better acquainted with the session topic or with each other

- **Group Discovery Questions:** a list of questions to encourage individual discovery or group participation

- **Personal Application Questions:** an aid to applying the knowledge gained through study to one's personal living (Note: These are important questions for group members to answer for themselves, even if they do not wish to discuss their responses in the meeting.)

- **Focus on Prayer:** suggestions for turning one's learning into prayer

- **Assignment:** activities or preparation to complete prior to the next session

Here are a few tips that can help you more effectively lead small-group studies:

- **Pray** for each group member, asking the Lord to help you create an open atmosphere where everyone will feel free to talk with one another and with you.

- **Encourage** group members to bring their Bibles as well as their texts to each session. This guide is based on the *New American Standard Bible,* Updated Edition, but it is good to have several translations on hand for purposes of comparison.

- **Start** and end on time. This is especially important for the first meeting because it will set the pattern for the rest of the sessions.

- **Begin** with prayer, asking the Holy Spirit to open hearts and minds and to give understanding so that truth will be applied.

- **Involve** everyone. As learners, we retain only 10 percent of what we hear; 20 percent of what we see; 65 percent of what we hear and see; but 90 percent of what we hear, see and do. Promote a relaxed environment. Arrange the chairs in a circle or semicircle. This allows eye contact among members and encourages dynamic discussion. Be relaxed in your own attitude and manner. Be willing to share yourself.

CHAPTER ONE
THE PREEMINENT ONE

Chapter Theme

Jesus Christ was no mere man—He is the full representation of and the human expression of God, superior to and exalted above anyone or anything.

Icebreaker

List one thing you have created (it could be something simple like a drawing or a recipe). Anything that originated with you in a sense was created by you. What kind of relationship does the thing you created have with you? How does that relate to your relationship with Christ?

Group Discovery Questions

1. What are some of the explanations offered for who Jesus Christ really was? (pp. 13-14)

2. Explain how Colossians 1:15 and Hebrews 1:3 show the deity of Christ. (pp. 15-17)

3. What did the apostle Paul mean when he described Jesus as "the firstborn of all creation"? (pp. 17-18)

4. What is Christ's inheritance? When and how will He take control of it? (pp. 17-18)

5. As the Creator, what did Christ create? What does that prove about Him? (pp. 19-20)

6. What current, active role does Christ have in relation to the universe? Explain. (pp. 20-21)

7. Describe Christ's relationship to the church. (pp. 22-24)

Practical Application Questions

1. Many cults deny the deity of Jesus Christ. In fact, they say that Jesus never claimed to be God. Is that true? Are you prepared to meet their challenge? What Scriptures would you use to show that Jesus did claim to be God? Always be ready to confront the false claims and assertions of those who pervert the truth. Ask God to give you the opportunity to share these truths with someone who opposes or is just questioning the deity of Christ.

2. In John 8:12 Jesus said, "I am the Light of the world; he who follows Me will not walk in the darkness, but will have the Light of life." We have the great opportunity of transmitting Christ's light to the world. How would you rate your success in reflecting His light to the unsaved world? Can unbelievers determine that you are a Christian by your behavior? Pray about your Christian walk. Ask God to help you reflect His glory.

Focus on Prayer

In light of what you have learned about Christ from this chapter, how have you failed to give Him the honor and glory due Him? Ask God to start you back on the path of loving Christ with all your heart, soul, mind and strength. Focus on one aspect of His preeminence each day and begin to praise the Lord for each one in your daily prayer time.

Assignment

If God were to become a man, what would He be like? The following answers have been proposed:

- He would be sinless.
- He would speak the greatest words ever spoken.
- He would exert a profound influence on human personality.
- He would work miracles with ease.
- He would be filled with love for others.

- He would exercise power over death.
- He would satisfy the spiritual hunger of men.

Jesus fulfilled every one of those characteristics. To see this for yourself, match the following verses with the corresponding characteristic (there are three verses for each characteristic): Matthew 8:23-27; 9:18-26; 11:28; Luke 4:32; 6:35; 7:22; 19:1-10; 21:33; 23:39-43; John 2:1-11,19-21; 7:46; 10:10; 11:5,32-44; 13:34; 14:27; 2 Corinthians 5:21; 1 Timothy 1:12-16; 1 Peter 2:22; 1 John 3:5.

CHAPTER TWO
GOD'S GLORIOUS PLAN

Chapter Theme

God chose and preordained who would be conformed to the image of Christ before the foundation of the world. Because of that glorious plan of salvation, all who love Him will give Him the honor and glory He deserves.

Icebreakers (Choose One)

1. When you take a vacation, how far in advance do you plan? What are some of the specific plans you make for your trip? Why are those things necessary? Since God is perfect, why do you suppose He needed to plan the salvation of His elect before the foundation of the world?

2. List some of the characteristics of an individual whom you find is easy to love. What about those whom you find difficult to love? With that in mind, what do you suppose motivated God to love those He chose to save?

Group Discovery Questions

1. What is the only source for genuine purpose and meaning in life? (p. 25)

2. Why did God pick the nation Israel to be His chosen people? What criteria does He use in choosing whom He will save? (p. 26)

3. Describe how Christ could be considered as the agent of our salvation. (pp. 27-28)

4. What was God's ultimate purpose in saving believers? (pp. 29-30)

5. Describe the extent of God's blessings for believers. (p. 31)

6. How does a believer receive his heavenly blessings? (p. 33)

7. What are the three kinds of election? Which one applies to God's choosing believers? Explain. (pp. 33-34)

8. What is the best way to reconcile the biblical truths of God's sovereign election and man's responsibility in choosing Jesus Christ? (pp. 34-35)

9. What did God want to accomplish in those He saved? Explain. (pp. 35-36)

10. What is the special relationship that only believers have to God and Christ? (pp. 36-37)

11. For what purpose does creation exist? Explain. (p. 37)

Practical Application Questions

1. We are to praise God because He is good. What specific characteristics of God's goodness do the following verses teach? Psalm 145:8-9,14-20; Matthew 5:45; John 3:16; Ephesians 2:4-5,8-9; Titus 3:5; Hebrews 6:7; James 5:11; and 1 John 4:10. How should you respond as a result?

2. Ephesians 1:4 tells us we are holy by virtue of our position in Christ. According to 1 Peter 1:15-16, 2 Peter 3:14 and 1 John 3:7, how are we to live in light of our position? What are the specific areas you need to work on to make you more set apart (holy) from sin unto God?

Focus on Prayer

Since God has blessed you with every spiritual blessing in the heavenly places in Christ, ask God to give you wisdom in applying those resources to each spiritual need you have. Remember, don't ask Him to give you what He already has, but do ask Him to guide you in the use of those resources.

Assignment

What gives you your sense of self-worth or value? Read through the first chapter of Ephesians and write down all that you are and all that you've been given as a Christian. Take some time to meditate on your list. Thank God for what He has given you and for making you His child.

CHAPTER THREE
IN THE LIKENESS OF MEN

Chapter Theme
Jesus Christ, the very Creator and Sustainer of the universe, condescended to become a creature so that He could save those whom God had chosen from before the foundation of the world.

Icebreaker
Suppose you had some vital information you wanted to communicate to your pet, whether it is a dog, a cat, a bird, or any other type of pet. What would be the best way you could communicate exactly your message? What else might your pet learn about you personally? When Christ humbled Himself to become a man, what else did He communicate to us besides the message of salvation?

Group Discovery Questions
1. Explain what Paul meant when he said that Jesus "existed in the form of God" (Phil. 2:6). (pp. 43-44)

2. What was the starting point of Christ's humiliation? Why is that significant? (p. 45)

3. Although Paul says that Christ "did not regard equality with God a thing to be grasped," what did Jesus continue to claim while He was on earth? Why? (pp. 45-46)

4. What does the Incarnation express about Christ? (p. 46)

5. What did Christ empty Himself of? What didn't He empty Himself of? Explain. (pp. 46-48)

6. As a result of His self-emptying, what role did Christ take on? (pp. 48-49)

7. In what ways was Christ identified with sinners? In what one significant way was Christ not identified with sinners? Explain. (p. 49)

8. How did Christ respond when He was put on trial for His life? (p. 50)

9. To what end did Christ's humility take Him? (pp. 50-51)

10. What would have been the logical outcome if some human devised a plan of salvation different from God's? Explain. (p. 51)

Practical Application Questions

1. In Philippians 2:5-8 we see how the Savior lived and died for the glory of God. The early nineteenth-century American preacher Gardiner Spring wrote, "The cross is the emblem of peace, but it is also an emblem of ignominy and suffering: it was so to the Saviour—it is so to his followers; nor do they refuse any of its forms of reproach and suffering, but willingly endure them for the name of Christ."[1] Christ said that those who come after Him must take up their cross and follow Him (see Matt. 16:24). In agreement with the example of Christ, have you taken up the cross of living for His honor and glory, no matter what?

2. It can be easy to let the great theological truths of Philippians 2:5-8 obscure the practical intent in its context. Those truths are but an illustration of the humble attitude that is to characterize every believer (see v. 5). The Puritan Thomas Watson observed, "Love is a humble grace; it does not walk abroad in state; it will creep upon its hands; it will stoop and submit to anything whereby it may be serviceable to Christ."[2] The love of Christ was such that He was humble enough to die on a cross— an excruciating obedience that brought salvation to mankind.

Consider whether you are willing to humble yourself for the sake of Christ and others.

Focus on Prayer

Jesus Christ gave up a great deal to come to earth to save you. Ask God to give you a greater love for Christ as a result of what He gave up for you. Each morning for the next week, meditate on one particular facet of His descent from His lofty position with God. As you do, offer praise to the One who gave up so much for you. Then give yourself and your day as an offering of service to Him.

Assignment

Try to imagine what life on earth must have been like for our Lord. He was constantly exposed to sinners and sin, yet how did He respond? As an exercise, pick any narrative section of a Gospel (a few chapters will do). As you read, note Jesus' response to sin. What is characteristic of each of His responses? How should His example lead you to respond when you find yourself in similar circumstances?

Notes

1. Gardiner Spring, *The Attraction of the Cross* (Edinburgh: Banner of Truth Trust, 1983), p. 192.
2. Thomas Watson, *All Things for Good* (Edinburgh: Banner of Truth Trust, 1986), p. 87.

CHAPTER FOUR
THE SUFFERING SERVANT

Chapter Theme
The Christian life is a call to glory through a journey of suffering. Our model of how to respond to suffering is Jesus Christ, and we need to follow His example.

Icebreaker
Are you currently enduring what you consider unjust suffering? What are the characteristics of your situation? How are you currently responding to the situation? Do you believe your responses are righteous? Where have you turned for help? Why?

Group Discovery Questions
1. Why can the Christian life be rightly considered a journey of suffering? (p. 56)

2. Why should Christians endure suffering? How does God use suffering in the lives of believers? (pp. 57-58)

3. What ought to be the believer's focus when he or she is in the midst of a trial? Why? (p. 58)

4. Why is Christ our example of unjust suffering? (p. 58)

5. How do we follow Christ's pattern of enduring suffering? (p. 59)

6. How did Christ react during His unjust trial and His crucifixion? (pp. 59-61)

7. What do believers forfeit when they retaliate to unjust suffering? What does that expose in the Christian? (p. 62)

Practical Application Questions
1. We often treat suffering as if it's to be avoided at all costs, yet it's often the best display of a life transformed by Christ. Rob-

ert Murray McCheyne, a Scottish minister of the early nineteenth century, said, "There is a great want about all Christians who have not suffered. Some flowers must be broken or bruised before they emit any fragrance."[1] Do you view afflictions, trials and sufferings as things to be avoided, or as the greatest opportunities to project the fragrance of a transformed life?

2. Your speech indicates the state of your heart—either the evil that's in it or the grace that dominates it. A. W. Tozer has written, "The fear that keeps us quiet when faith and love and loyalty cry out for us to speak is surely evil and must be judged as evil before the bar of eternal justice."[2] Jesus' speech in His time of trial revealed a heart filled with the grace of God—He spoke no evil but answered with the truth. Does your speech show the grace of God, even when faced with a severe trial?

Focus on Prayer

While the example of Christ's suffering ought to hearten us in times of persecution, perhaps even more it ought to make us grateful for His willingness to suffer for us sinners (see Rom. 5:8). Take time now to express your gratitude to our Lord for His willingness to suffer on our behalf.

Assignment

Review the section that details Christ's reaction to those who persecuted and crucified Him (pp. 59-64). If you are currently enduring a trial or are suffering unjust persecution to some degree, compare your reactions to those of the Lord. What attitudes and actions do you need to change to reflect the spirit of Christ? Make a list of those things and seek to respond in those ways this week. At the end of the week, examine your attitude toward your situation. Has it improved? If so, in what ways?

Notes

1. Robert Murray McCheyne, cited in *More Gathered Gold: A Treasury of Quotations for Christians*, edited by John Blanchard (Welwyn, UK: Evangelical Press, 1986), p. 315.
2. A. W. Tozer, cited in *Signposts: A Collection of Sayings from A.W. Tozer*, edited by Harry Verploegh (Wheaton, IL: Victor Books, 1988), p. 195.

CHAPTER FIVE
OUR LOVING SUBSTITUTE

Chapter Theme

Before salvation, all believers deserved to die because they had violated God's holy standard. But God, because of His great love, provided us with a Substitute who would die in our place and pay the penalty for our sins, thus satisfying God's justice.

Icebreaker

What is it like to be in debt to someone or some institution? Are you now or have you ever been in a situation where paying off the debt seemed impossible? Describe the burden that accompanies a debt. Did you ever feel that way regarding your sin before you were a Christian? Explain.

Group Discovery Questions

1. Left to his own resources, what can man hope to accomplish with regard to his own salvation? What is the only alternative? (p. 66)

2. What is man's basic problem? Explain. (pp. 67-68)

3. What is the standard God has established that man cannot live up to? (p. 68)

4. Describe the condition of all believers before they were saved. What is the driving force that causes unbelievers to live in such a manner? (pp. 69-70)

5. How would you characterize the importance of God's love to His plan of salvation? Explain. (pp. 70-71)

6. What would have happened had Christ not willed to take our sin and accept its punishment? (p. 72)

7. Define and explain the four terms that describe the richness of our salvation in Christ. (p. 72)

8. Explain the two Greek legal terms that define redemption. Which one best describes the New Testament idea of redemption? Why? (p. 73)

9. What was the price of our redemption? Explain. (p. 75)

10. What is the result of redemption for the Christian? According to Colossians 2:14, how did God accomplish it? (pp. 75-76)

11. According to 2 Corinthians 5:17-21, what are the benefits of a person's reconciliation to God? (pp. 78-79)

12. What is the goal of our reconciliation? (pp. 79-80)

Practical Application Questions

1. Read Ephesians 2:1-3. As you do, substitute personal pronouns in the appropriate places. How does that make you want to respond to God? With those verses in mind, are we to view the unsaved as our enemies or as prisoners of the enemy? Why? How can having a proper perspective of the unsaved change our attitudes toward them? Do you have an unsaved acquaintance whom you've been treating as an enemy? Ask the Lord to help you see him or her as someone who needs the gospel.

2. Read Romans 6:16-23. Are Christians and non-Christians free to live as they please? Explain your answer using Paul's teaching in this text. Believers have been set free from bondage to sin. Does any part of your life reflect that you are still living as though you're under bondage? After you have confessed and repented of that sin, seek out another believer to whom you can be accountable.

Focus on Prayer

Considering all that Christ has done for you, what should be your response? Take this moment to praise your Lord for all He has done in accomplishing your redemption. Ask Him to forgive you for neglecting the priority of your relationship to Him and for your weak love to Him. Thank Him that because of His accomplished redemption, all your sins, including your weak love, have been forgiven and removed as far as the east is from the west. Finally, ask Him to help you seek after Him—to base all your thoughts and activities toward accomplishing His will.

Assignment

Even though all your sins have been forgiven, it is important to confess your sins before God. Why? What do the following passages teach about the importance of confession: Psalms 32:1-5; 38:17-18; 66:18; Proverbs 28:13-14; 1 Corinthians 11:23-32? Why is confession important before you study God's Word?

CHAPTER SIX
THE PERFECT SACRIFICE

Chapter Theme
The death of Christ became the great and final sacrifice that accomplished for eternity what all the other Old Testament sacrifices never could.

Icebreaker
What is the usual reason most people buy something new to replace something old? Does it mean that what is now old was bad? What would you willingly pay if you could replace all the old things in your house with new things that would never wear out and would never need to be replaced?

Group Discovery Questions
1. What did the Old Covenant constantly remind the people of? (p. 82)

2. Although it couldn't provide access to God, what did the law accomplish for the people? Explain. (p. 83)

3. What was the law unable to do regarding sin? What did it remind the people of? (pp. 83-84)

4. Explain how Christ's sacrifice fulfilled God's design. (pp. 85-86)

5. What did Christ's sacrifice do to the Old Covenant system? (p. 86)

6. What does our experience teach us about our practical holiness? (p. 87)

7. Why was Christ's sacrifice the only one that could appease God's wrath? (p. 88)

8. What did Christ's sacrifice on the cross do to Satan? (pp. 88-89)

9. What was the prophecy that Jeremiah made regarding the New Covenant? (p. 89)

Practical Application Questions

1. Have you taken something that should be an expression of faith and turned it into a ritual that is devoid of faith? Have you been on a Bible-reading schedule and lost sight of the One you are seeking to follow? Have you let your mind wander as a group of believers is praying? Such obstacles to true communication with God are bound to appear, but if they are the norm in your spiritual activity, maybe you are in the rut of ritualism. If you are on a reading schedule, make sure you allow enough time to meditate on what you are reading. As you listen to the prayers of others, strive to concentrate and agree in your heart with what is said. Whatever you do, don't be one who honors God with your lips while your heart is far from Him (see Isa. 29:13 and Matt. 15:8).

2. How sensitive are you to your own sin? When you are tempted to sin, do you force yourself to remember how God views sin, or do you rationalize away the consequences of sin? Don't ever forget that God hates sin and He will deal with it in your life if you persist in it. In your ongoing battle with sin, keep in mind the following:

- Judge and discipline yourself for godliness (see 1 Cor. 11:31-32; 1 Tim. 4:7-8).

- Confess your sin regularly (see Ps. 32:1-5; 1 John 1:8-2:2).

- Yield your life daily to the Holy Spirit's control (see Rom. 8:11-14; Gal. 5:16).

- Realize the cost to God to redeem you from sin (see 1 Pet. 1:17-2:3).

Focus on Prayer

Take this time to thank God for His redemptive plan and for the willingness of Christ to sacrifice Himself for you. Praise Him for the permanence of His plan.

Assignment

Christians have the distinct advantage over the Old Testament saints of living on this side of the cross. To gain a greater appreciation of this privilege, along with a better understanding of the Old Covenant, read Hebrews 7–10. As you do, read the Old Testament texts that the writer of Hebrews interprets. Make special note of those that are specifically fulfilled in the New Covenant.

CHAPTER SEVEN
THE NAME ABOVE ALL NAMES

Chapter Theme
The gospel is not complete without the exaltation of Christ. He who was the perfect sacrifice for sin was raised up from the dead and exalted to God's right hand to prove the effectiveness of His redemptive work.

Icebreaker
Without considering the spiritual realm, who has authority over you? How do they maintain that authority? Does anyone abuse that authority? Why? To whom do you give respect grudgingly? To whom do you give it gladly? Why?

Group Discovery Questions

1. What historical event is arguably the pinnacle of redemptive history? Why? (p. 98)

2. What would have been the logical outcome had not Christ been raised from the dead? (pp. 98-99)

3. What does the resurrection of Christ prove? (p. 99)

4. Why was death powerless to hold Christ? (pp. 99-100)

5. Hebrews 1:3 tells us that after Christ ascended to heaven He sat down at God's right hand. What does that event signify? (pp. 101-102)

6. What name did God bestow on Christ when He was exalted? What is the significance of that name? (pp. 103-104)

7. According to Philippians 2:10, what is the only appropriate response to Christ? (pp. 105-106)

8. Who are called to worship Christ? Explain. (pp. 106-107)

Practical Application Questions

1. The humiliation and exaltation of Christ are lessons for all believers: "As Christ ceased not to be a King because He was a servant, nor to be a lion because He was like a lamb, nor to be God because He was made a man, nor to be a judge because He was judged; so a man does not lose his honour by humility, but he shall be honoured for his humility."[1] Does your life demonstrate a Christlike humility that God will delight to honor by exaltation?

2. A major theological issue of our time concerns whether faith in Christ necessarily requires evident repentance from sin. Some have said that to require repentance from sin as a part of the gospel message—and as a ground of assurance of saving faith—is a form of legalism. Yet the first sermon of Christ was, "Repent, for the kingdom of heaven is at hand" (Matt. 4:17). Among His final words were, "Repentance for forgiveness of sins should be proclaimed in His name to all nations, beginning from Jerusalem" (Luke 24:47). The apostles also emphasized repentance: when Peter was asked what his hearers needed to do to be saved, he said, "Repent, and each one of you be baptized in the name of Jesus Christ for the forgiveness of your sins" (Acts 2:38). Does repentance characterize your life? Do you realize its necessity for a daily walk with Christ?

Focus on Prayer

In your daily walk, how often do you acknowledge Christ as Lord of your life? Do you honor Him as God—as the sovereign ruler of all life's situations? If you are a true Christian, you will want to do so. To help you see yourself under His divine hand, ask the Lord to constantly remind you of His presence throughout the day. As He does, take that moment to acknowledge His rulership and to confess any sin you may be dealing with at that moment.

Assignment

As a complement to the focus on prayer above, to help remind yourself of the Lord's presence, post in prominent places key verses you want to make a part of your life. (Sample posting spots include your refrigerator, on your desk or workbench, on the dashboard of your car, on the washing machine, or next to the sewing machine.) Also, do not neglect your daily study of His Word. As you fill your mind with His truths, He will use them in your life at the appropriate times.

Note

1. Henry Smith, cited in *A Puritan Golden Treasury* (Edinburgh: Banner of Truth Trust, 1977), p. 149.

CHAPTER EIGHT
AT THE RIGHT HAND OF GOD

Chapter Theme
The final step in Christ's exaltation is His current ministry of intercession for Christians. As a result, believers need never doubt their salvation or be discouraged by their sin.

Icebreaker
When someone comes to you with a problem seeking your advice, how do you respond? Do you keep your counsel purely on a technical level, or do you try to get involved physically and emotionally in helping them solve their problem? How much do you share your own life's experiences in the process? How often do you wish you had the resources to take care of their problem?

Group Discovery Questions

1. Name some of the pressures Christians face in our society. What is the only way to truly deal with those pressures? (p. 112)

2. In what two areas does Satan often attack believers? Why? (pp. 112-113)

3. Explain how Christ is able to "sympathize with our weaknesses" (see Heb. 4:15). (pp. 113-114)

4. Why was Jesus faced with degrees of temptation that we will never experience? (pp. 114-115)

5. According to Hebrews 4:16, how does Jesus' sympathy go beyond anything man can offer another person? (pp. 116-117)

6. Describe Christ's role as an advocate before God. (p. 118)

7. What is the security of the believer's salvation? (pp. 118-120)

Practical Application Questions

1. Times of discouragement can be destructive to Christians. That's when we really need someone to lean on, but sometimes a loving brother or sister in Christ is not available. Even if someone were, Christ wants you to lean on Him first—because He is the best one to deal with your pain. To help you through such times, memorize 1 Corinthians 10:13: "No temptation has overtaken you but such as is common to man; and God is faithful, who will not allow you to be tempted beyond what you are able, but with the temptation will provide the way of escape also, so that you will be able to endure it."

2. It is vital that you be honest with God about your sins. Any attempt to hide them from Him is futile because He knows all about them even before you do. Do you spend an adequate amount of time admitting your sins in detail to God when you pray? Do you express true penitence and humility over your sins? What can you gain by doing so?

Focus on Prayer

Read 2 Corinthians 5:17-21. According to Paul, all Christians have been given the ministry of reconciliation. What are some ways you personally can be involved as an ambassador for Christ? Based on the fact that you have peace with God, what has to be an integral part of your ministry? Make a list of people you know whom you'd like to see at peace with God. Begin praying that God will use you to bring about their reconciliation to Him.

Assignment

Since you now have access into God's presence and stand in His grace, with what attitude should you approach God? Look up the following verses: Hebrews 4:14-16; 10:12-22; 1 John 3:18-21; 4:17; 5:14. Why is it possible for us to have that attitude? List some reasons that explain why sometimes we don't approach God in that way. Read 1 John 1:9. Remember, it is confession of sin that enables us to keep our consciences clean (see Heb. 10:22) and be obedient to God. Although we can approach Him confidently, we must also approach Him with humility (see Jas. 4:10).

CHAPTER NINE
LOVE AND OBEDIENCE

Chapter Theme
True love to Christ will be proven by the level of one's obedience to Him.

Icebreaker
Have you ever found yourself in a situation where you denied the reality of your faith before a group of unbelievers? Has there been an occasion when you failed to stand up for Christ when His name was being disparaged by a similar group of people? How did you feel?

Group Discovery Questions

1. Why do many people today lack conviction about what their priorities ought to be? How has that mindset infiltrated the church? (pp. 126-127)

2. What steps led to Peter's denial of Christ? Explain. (pp. 129-130)

3. What caused Peter to repent of his sin? (p. 131)

4. Why did Peter decide to return to his former life as a fisherman? (p. 132)

5. What lesson did Christ have to give the disciples a second time? Why? (pp. 132-134)

6. When a true Christian fails temporarily in His love to Christ, what can he be assured of? (p. 134)

7. In Christ's dialogue with Peter (John 21:15-17), what did our Lord want Peter to understand? (pp. 135-136)

8. What is the cost that is attached to loving Christ? (p. 136)

Practical Application Questions

1. Analyze your spiritual preparedness. Are you like Peter, prepared for the big tests but unprepared for the small ones? What can you do to be better prepared for the small tests? Our involuntary responses reveal our true character and its weaknesses. In Peter's case, what led to his failure in the small tests? How might you turn those weaknesses of Peter's character into strengths in you? Commit yourself to building spiritual character. As you do, you will find your involuntary responses revealing your strengths instead of your weaknesses.

2. Review the dialogue between Christ and Peter (John 21:15-17). Determine the most recent occasion where you have failed to identify yourself as a Christian in the midst of unbelievers. How would you respond to the Lord's questioning of the reality of your love for Him? Could you answer like Peter, or would the Lord be correct in questioning even the reality of your affection for Him? If you are a true Christian, you will stand up for Christ and prove your love to Him no matter the cost.

Focus on Prayer

Thank the Lord that in spite of your weak love, He always loves you and is willing to restore you. Take this time to confess and repent of those times you failed to stand for Him.

Assignment

Peter's repentance was born out of his recognition of Christ and his understanding that he sinned against his Lord. When you sin, what makes you repent? Do you repent out of sorrow for having sinned against Christ, or is it the result of knowing that as a believer you should repent of sin? Can the latter be true repentance if it isn't motivated by the former? Look up the following verses: Isaiah 6:5, Daniel 9:5-7, Micah 7:9 and Luke 15:17-20. What do each of those verses teach about the motivation for repentance? Read Psalm 51 and meditate on the verses that reveal David's repentant heart. Memorize the verses that are most meaningful to you. Use them to help motivate true repentance from your heart each time the Lord convicts you of sin.

CHAPTER TEN
IN PURSUIT OF OUR FIRST LOVE

Chapter Theme

Your allegiance and love to Christ demand a lifelong commitment. That is the only way a believer will ever become like Him.

Icebreaker

When was the last time you ran in a race? Many of you will have to go back to a time when you were still in school. What do you remember most about the race? How did you finish? Did you run with all your energy?

Group Discussion Questions

1. While Paul's relationship to Christ was the passion of his life (Phil. 3:10-11), how did he assess that relationship? (pp. 140-141)

2. What is the Christian's goal in this life? What does it require? (p. 142)

3. In keeping the correct focus, what two things must a believer do in his pursuit of Christ? Explain. (pp. 142-143)

4. What motivated Paul in his pursuit of Christ? What did he avoid? (pp. 143-144)

5. What kind of attitude should every believer have regarding his or her own spiritual condition? What will God do if you have the wrong attitude? (p. 144)

6. What is a hallmark of true spirituality? How will that affect our behavior? (pp. 145-146)

7. What are some specific benefits of living in anticipation of Christ's return? (pp. 146-147)

8. What will happen when God transforms our bodies? (pp. 147-148)

9. How would you describe the inheritance we will one day receive from God? (pp. 148-149)

Practical Application Questions

1. Encumbrances and obstacles slow a runner considerably in any race. So it is with spiritual growth. Hebrews 12:1 says, "Let us . . . lay aside every encumbrance and the sin which so easily entangles us, and let us run with endurance the race that is set before us." Examine your life to determine what may be holding you back in your spiritual race. It may be possessions or pleasures that are not wrong in themselves but perhaps distract you from spiritual things. Also, ask God to reveal any sin in your life and then confess and forsake it.

2. A tremendous amount of self-discipline is necessary to run a race effectively. Paul said, "Do you not know that those who run in a race all run, but only one receives the prize? Run in such a way that you may win. Everyone who competes in the games exercises self-control in all things. . . . Therefore I run in such a way, as not without aim" (1 Cor. 9:24-26). Do you approach your Christian life with the same intensity as an athlete training for an event? Write down some ways in which you can "train yourself to be godly. For physical training is of some value, but godliness has value for all things, holding promise for both the present life and the life to come" (1 Tim. 4:7-8, *NIV*).

Focus on Prayer

Only you can give the effort in pursuing Christ, but God will certainly uphold your resolve if you ask Him. Beginning today, ask God to daily convict you of those areas in which you fall short in your love to Christ. Take time each day to meditate on and praise the Lord for His character and some specific work that He accomplished for you. Get to know your Lord better simply by spending time in prayer with Him each day.

Assignment

Review the nine directives that Thomas Vincent gave for building up your love to Christ. Write them down on a piece of paper that you can keep in your Bible. Begin to make each one a daily reality in your life. Don't ever leave your first love—keep on pursuing Him each day until the day you meet Him in heaven.

SCRIPTURE INDEX

Subject Index

MORE PRACTICAL BIBLICAL TRUTHS FROM JOHN MACARTHUR

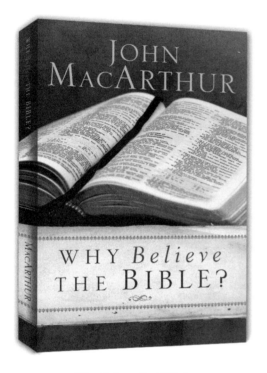

Why Believe the Bible?
John MacArthur
ISBN: 08307.45645
ISBN: 978.08307.45647

With the authority of the Bible being questioned by many in today's society and the need for solid, biblical teaching, the timeliness of *Why Believe the Bible?* is apparent. The esteemed Bible teacher John MacArthur examines many common questions about the Bible in this practical examination of the authority, infallibility and trustworthiness of God's Word. Readers will come to desire a deeper Bible study time after reading "Can We Really Take God's Word for It?" "What Does God's Word Do for You?" and "How to Get the Most from God's Word." For new Christians and those wanting to brush up on the basic truths of the Bible, *Why Believe the Bible?* features a Bible reading plan with study tips and an appendix with helpful tools for Bible study.